Tibetan Meditation

Practical teachings and step-by-step exercises on how
to live in harmony, peace and happiness

Tarthang Tulku

Tibetan Meditation

Practical teachings and step-by-step exercises on
how to live in harmony, peace and happiness

DUNCAN BAIRD PUBLISHERS

LONDON

Tibetan Meditation
Tarthang Tulku

First published in the United Kingdom and
Ireland in 2006 by
Duncan Baird Publishers Ltd
Sixth Floor, Castle House
75–76 Wells Street
London W1T 3QH

Editor: Judy Barratt
Designer: Rachel Cross
Managing designer: Manisha Patel
Commissioned artwork: Cathie Bleck
Commissioned photography: Matthew Ward

British Library Cataloguing-in-Publication Data:
A CIP record for this book is available from the
British Library

ISBN 1-84483-206-6

10 9 8 7 6 5 4 3 2 1

Typeset in Spectrum
Color reproduction by Scanhouse, Malaysia
Printed by Imago, Singapore

Tibetan Meditation is sourced with kind
permission from the following books and
articles:
*Gesture of Balance: A Guide to Awareness, Self-healing,
    and Meditation* Tarthang Tulku (Berkeley:
    Dharma Publishing, 1977)
Hidden Mind of Freedom Tarthang Tulku (Berkeley:
    Dharma Publishing, 1981)
Openness Mind Tarthang Tulku (Berkeley:
    Dharma Publishing, 1978)
The Spade Sage: A Jataka Tale (Berkeley: Dharma
    Publishing, 2004)
Mandala Gardens (Berkeley: Dharma Publishing,
    1991)
Mastering Successful Work Tarthang Tulku
    (Berkeley: Dharma Publishing, 1994)
Kum Nye Relaxation, Parts I and II Tarthang Tulku
    (Berkeley: Dharma Publishing, 1978)
Bringing the Teachings Alive: Crystal Mirror 4 (Revised)
    (Berkeley: Dharma Publishing, 2004)
"Cultivating the Seven Gestures," *Gesar Magazine*
    11(4): 26–29

Dedicated to the unbounded freedom of the human mind
and to the power of meditation that opens our hearts
to the blessings of beauty and inner peace.

"Every single thought, every moment of experience, has
a silent nature within it that we can contact directly. If we
understand this silent, meditative quality, there is no need
to fight or subdue anything or anyone."
Tarthang Tulku

CONTENTS

FOREWORD

Meditation is the foundation of self-development and well-being. Gradually, almost imperceptibly, meditation transforms the quality of everyday life, stimulating creativity, exercising mental capacities, and integrating body and mind. Through meditation, we can open ourselves to a path of self-knowledge that leads ultimately to enlightenment. This path was taken twenty-five hundred years ago by the Buddha: his penetrating investigation into the causes of unhappiness and the means to perfect health culminated in the full realization of human potential. After his liberation the Buddha taught that no matter what our background or present lifestyle, this awareness cannot fade with the passage of time.

The teachings of the Buddha invite us to develop our knowing capacity to the fullest and provide us with methods we can use in transforming everyday experience. A number of different meditation approaches may be found in this book, including breathing, mantra, and visualization. Explore them all to find the best for you—each leads toward the realization of the enlightened mind.

Understanding the mind is at the heart of all Eastern philosophies and religions. They suggest that our experience comes from the mind, by means of the mind, and for the mind, and urge us to develop this understanding within our own lives. We need to encourage ourselves to learn from everything we do. Firm confidence in experience itself is especially important in these times because there are so few genuine spiritual teachers to guide us.

We can develop a close, reliable friendship with our experience. As this friendship grows, we discover that transcendence is not found somewhere beyond, or in some other time: whatever happens in our lives can serve to embody enlightenment. Even the density of confusion and pain can be transmuted into contemplation and fullness. We need simply to relax, allow our breathing to become calm, and watch our experience mindfully, without judgment. In this way we learn to foster lightness, joy, and compassion instead of resistance and disappointment. As meditation develops, we become naturally cheerful and find meaning in all that we do.

How do you know when you have attained the highest realization? Sometimes after students have had an experience they consider enlightenment, they ask their teachers what to do next. But when you are free, you do not ask what to do or what not to do. Liberation is perfect knowledge of the truth, unobscured by judgments of right or wrong. Once we are enlightened, we participate continuously in the perfection of being.

This book offers some introductory discussions of the basic practices in meditation and awareness as they relate to present-day life in the West. Certain themes in these chapters overlap, but this repetition is intended to provide a foundation for developing an increasingly deep understanding of practice. Although the ideas and practices are specifically oriented to the experience of Western people, they are founded on the many different stages and paths of the Buddhist tradition as preserved by the Nyingma lineage.

In Tibet the Nyingma followers interacted with many different types of people—not concentrating on exclusively monastic orientation—and Nyingma masters have always included people of different attainments and lifestyles. I have tried to retain this adaptable and open-minded character, and therefore hope that this book can offer something of value to people of different positions and interests. My main concern is that the discussions help people to establish a path of growth that is right for them, so that they may take care of themselves in the midst of a troubled world.

CHAPTER I

UNDERSTANDING MEDITATION

principles, philosophies & aims

Meditation is absolutely natural, but still we need some explanation or instruction with which to begin. How does one start to meditate? Someone who is not accustomed to meditation often feels that it is something foreign, unusual, or unnatural. He or she may view meditation as something outside oneself, separate from the person, an experience to be achieved, or another facet of Eastern thought to study and explore. Meditation, though, is not necessarily foreign, separate, or external. Meditation is within your own mind—the whole nature of your mind can be meditation.

In this chapter we place these notions in the context of Tibetan Buddhism. We discover the principles of Dharma, and the concepts of Samsara and Shunyata. We think about what we are aiming for through meditation and, in doing so, take the first steps to preparing our minds for a new way of living.

THE WAY OF TIBETAN
MEDITATION

Almost all spiritual disciplines practice some form of meditation. Ordinarily, meditation is viewed as a form of thinking used in combination with words, images, or concepts—but meditation is not thinking about something. The meditative experience may seem subjective—my consciousness, my awareness. But as we look further into the meditative state, we find that awareness is neither subjective nor objective; it also cannot be conceptually analyzed. Awareness is a natural openness that takes place when the mind is left to function freely on its own—with no interruptions, distractions, or expectations.

Meditative awareness is like completely open space. But not space as we commonly understand it, because awareness is not a place, nor does it have any particular form or shape. This space is neither outside the body nor inside the mind. It is not mental or physical, and yet, at the same time, it is a deep, integrated sense of stillness, openness, and balance—which is the experience of meditation itself.

Traditionally, beginning meditation involves certain practices, such as intense concentration, the visualization of various images, or the chanting of mantras. Teachers emphasize different practices depending on the needs of the student. For example, a teacher may tell one student to go alone to a quiet place and be completely silent for half an hour or forty-five minutes, and he may tell another to go to the mountains or ocean and chant very loudly. Someone else may be instructed to gaze at the sky and just be open. Others may be given devotional or ritual practices.

Generally, however, our practice should be whatever calms and relaxes us—whatever works best for the development of stillness and concentration. Meditation helps us to be calm and happy—to enjoy life, to be cheerful, and to deal effectively with both our physical and mental problems. Our lives become balanced when we are able to integrate whatever we experience with our meditation. We can include our joy and happiness, as well as our anger, resentment, frustration, and unhappiness—all the emotions that we feel throughout the day. We can turn all our emotions into the relaxation and calmness of meditation.

In the beginning meditation seems simple—to be quiet, still, calm, and relaxed, and perhaps to follow specific instructions. But gradually, as we refine our meditation, we realize that meditation involves much more than just relaxing and dealing with our thoughts and emotions. Meditation is actually a process of seeking truth or understanding, of trying to discover the nature of existence, and of the human mind. To discover such knowledge we have to go extremely deeply into meditation, and find out who we really are.

So simply, how do you meditate? First of all, the body must be very still, very quiet. Physically relax your muscles and let go of all your tension. Then sit in a comfortable position and stay completely still, not moving at all. Breathe very softly and gently—inhale and exhale slowly and smoothly. As much as you can, completely relax so that your entire nervous system becomes calm. Then quiet the mind; still your thoughts through inner silence. There are various ways to do this, but as too many instructions may be distracting, just naturally relax your body, breath, and mind. The body becomes still, the breath balanced, and the mind and senses peaceful. At this time you deeply feel and enjoy your senses coming alive. You can see that meditation is not a difficult task or something foreign or imported—it is a part of your nature.

There is no need to try to accomplish some goal, as trying itself becomes an obstacle to relaxation. Pushing yourself too hard, or attempting to follow a rigid set of instructions, may cause problems—for when you exert too much effort, you can find yourself caught between getting something and not getting it, making internal reports to yourself while trying to be silent. When you try to conceptually experience the "perfect meditation," you may end up creating endless internal conflicts or inner dialogues.

Because concepts are necessary in introducing meditation, from the beginning the meditator is separated from the experience. But when you become involved in the actual practice of meditation, you find that meditation goes far beyond conceptualization. If you continue to relax and calm your mind, eventually no effort at all will be needed for your meditation.

When you are just learning to meditate, it is best to experience yourself totally, without rejecting or excluding any part of yourself. All of your thoughts and feelings can be a part of your meditation—you can taste each one, then gradually move on.

In this way you can begin to discover the various subtle layers and states of the mind. The mind simply observes its own natural process; every thought, desire, and motivation is a natural aid to this basic type of meditation. On the relative level there are still distinctions of good and bad, but when you realize a meditative state, you no longer perceive relative discriminations as accurately defining experience. Meditation transcends dualism. Whatever you experience can be seen as perfect, for the quality of perfection lies within your mind, not in anything external.

When memories or discomforts arise, you may feel a little uneasy, but this feeling will pass if you do not mentally hold on to any thought in particular. Just remain very loose and quiet and do not think "about" meditation. Simply accept yourself. You are not trying to learn meditation; you are the meditation. Your entire body, breath, thoughts, senses, and awareness—your total being—are all part of the meditation. You do not have to worry about losing it. Your entire energy-field is a part of the meditation, so you do not need to follow any specific instructions or worry about achieving a particular experience.

A famous Tibetan lama once said of meditation, "The best water is rocky water." As water flows over rocks, its quality improves and is purified. So the best meditation is one that is flowing and free—with nothing to hold on to—for once we hold a position, we are brought to a standstill by our grasping. How much more beautiful is the freedom to flow to the higher meditative states! When another master was asked, "When you are concentrating, where is your concentration?" He answered that there was no subject, no position, no goal.

As we experience this deeper level of meditation, we find that the nature of mind is meditation. And this, itself, is actually the enlightened experience. This experience is free from everything, and yet at the same time, it manifests all and everything. This, itself, is liberation.

SAMSARA AND THE DHARMA

If we look honestly at our everyday lives, what do we see? All experience is impermanent. No matter what we do or think, in time we will age, losing our vitality and health; eventually we will die. We can no more change this than we can prevent the sun from shining or the seasons from following their age-old cycle. Yet it is difficult for us to accept this truth.

Moving restlessly from experience to experience, we seek pleasure and try to avoid suffering. But even while pleasant feelings are fresh, they are unstable. In every situation enjoyment is eventually followed by disappointment. Precious new possessions gradually lose their attraction; a relationship with a new love sours as we come to know the idiosyncrasies of our partner. Even our children, for whom we hope so much, fail to meet our expectations.

We may seek wealth and success, hoping that they will solve our problems, and be drawn into projects, thoughts, and emotions that consume both time and energy. But our fantasies, however colorful, are seldom realized. Even if we make many sacrifices and reach our goals, something still seems lacking.

Eventually it becomes clear that our lives are not productive or beneficial for ourselves or the world. Like a dream animal we run through a desert pursuing a mirage. The more we run, the hotter we become; the drier and more depleted our energy, the more vivid the mirage appears. Running itself intensifies our craving.

In Buddhism our ordinary existence is called *samsara*. There is really no way that we can "fix" *samsara*, so that it becomes fully satisfying. As long as we are caught within it, we will be subject to its cycles of hope and fear, enjoyment and frustration, pleasure and pain. Sometimes we refuse to admit this. "Surely things will get better soon," we say to ourselves, putting off any attempt to bring about change. At other times we develop a pessimistic attitude: "I can't possibly change anything, so why try?" Indeed, it may seem hopeless, this samsaric existence. Where can we go that unhappiness does not follow like a shadow? Yet if we resign ourselves to disappointment, we will have lost a priceless opportunity.

The teachings of Buddhism, called the Dharma, tell us that to understand the hopelessness of *samsara* is to enter the path to *nirvana*, or liberation from suffering. This path carries us directly to the heart of *samsara* and teaches us to transform it into peace. When we follow the Dharma, our self-concepts, desires, and negative habits themselves provide the energy that fuels our spiritual growth. Every aspect of every situation becomes a process of training, learning, and understanding. The teachings become a silent song—a thread running through every moment—leading us to greater knowledge and awakening.

Therefore, encourage yourself to study the Dharma and realize its wisdom in your daily life. From the moment you wake up each day—and even during sleep—make every sensation and thought your spiritual practice. You can contact the teachings not only on the level of words and concepts, but internally, within daily experience. Your own frustration can push you toward a way to ease all pain and conflict. The impermanence of everything that matters to you, the transience of the relationships and things you most cherish, can inspire you to search for something that cannot be shaken loose or taken from you. And when you have found this great power and direction through the teachings, you will no longer have to search for satisfaction: you will find all you need within your own heart.

WHAT IS *SHUNYATA*?

The word *shunyata* (Tibetan: stong-pa-nyid) combines the words *shunya* (stong-pa), meaning "empty," and *ta* (nyid), meaning "state of being," or "-ness." *Shunya* means "empty" in the sense of "clear," or "absolute openness." It has nothing to stand on, either inside or outside; it is completely non-dual, not taking any position whatsoever. Therefore, everything past, present, or future becomes unified, and space, time, and matter become inseparable. When we say *shunyata* means "empty-ness," the "-ness" implies some quality or some description: it is distinguished from something else or implies some negation. But these are only our human interpretations, and this negation is only verbal. *Shunya*, or total openness, has nothing to do with positive or negative connotations. *Shunya* means: I cannot grasp it, I cannot see it, I cannot touch it, I cannot smell, interpret, or experience it. There is no "me" grasping, seeing, smelling, or experiencing. *Shunyata* has nothing to do with form or formlessness. It does not deny or accept the physicality of material substance, nor does it describe things comparatively as existent or non-existent. It is not that kind of emptiness. Everything is emptiness. Emptiness is everything.

The teaching of *shunyata* originally comes from the Buddha. After the Buddha was enlightened under the Bodhi tree, he thought to himself, "No one will be able to understand this supreme knowledge, therefore I will not be able to teach it to anyone. This is the nature of *shunyata*." So he silently decided to live in the forest, until the rulers of the heaven realms begged him to turn the Wheel of the Dharma so that suffering sentient beings could hear this precious teaching. Presenting the Buddha with many auspicious offerings—a beautiful golden wheel, an umbrella, a conch shell, cymbals, and so on—they said, "You cannot be silent. Please turn the Wheel of the Dharma." So at Bodh Gaya, before presenting the teachings verbally at Sarnath, the Buddha conveyed to a few great beings the significance of *shunyata*.

Shunyata has four or five general qualities: *zab-pa* (zab-pa) means "profound;" *zhiwa* (zhi-ba) means "great peace;" *odsalwa* (od-gsal-ba) means "great clarity" or "lucency;" *todral* (sprol-bral)—generally translated as "voidness"—means "beyond imaginative activity," a freedom which has nothing to do with conceptual ideas, symbols or gestures; and *dusmaye* (dus-ma-byas) means "unconditioned," "uncompounded," "uncreated." These five qualities of *shunyata* are like nectar, but, as the Buddha himself said, "I found this vast knowledge, but if I reveal these teachings, no one will be able to understand them either verbally or symbolically." This was the basic problem: *shunyata* has no characteristics and no essence, so the Buddha could not point it out anywhere. *Shunyata* cannot be described or explained—it cannot even be experienced, either physically through the senses, or conceptually through images and thoughts. So how can we contact this deep teaching?

First, there is no way we can interpret *shunyata*. We cannot say anything about it, for none of our ideas, concepts, mental activity, and intuitions can explain it. All we can do is chop down and completely destroy every position, throw away everything, and unmask everything, then let our minds become totally silent, peaceful, and clear—become the experience, become *shunyata*. If we truly and completely let go of everything, our whole being becomes the nature of open space. Within this open awareness or lucidity, between the thoughts, before the next concept forms, there is no subject and no object, no experience and no experiencer.

THE MEDITATION
MIND——HOW TO BEGIN

Buddha's teaching is a way of life. It is a path for living a balanced, peaceful, and useful life: a path that provides us with a way out of the endless series of problems and struggles we face in life. We can discover this path in meditation, a way that opens us to the meaning of enlightenment.

When meditating in this simple, accepting way, the meditative quality gradually becomes more pronounced, and its experience more immediate. After each meditation the light of this experience will remain and strengthen with practice. Meditation just comes of itself, like the morning sun; inner awareness, once touched upon, radiates naturally. But finding this inner awareness needs daily practice, so it is important to set aside time for meditation.

As you persevere in your practice, you will know whether you are on the right path, and whether your meditation is effective, by examining your life. When your mind is peaceful and more loving, when your emotions are steady and even, and your life is going smoothly, then you know that you are making progress.

The inner quiet that arises from meditation relieves the stress of these times of rapid change, when it is so easy to lose our sense of stability and balance. Balance is central even in our relationship to the spiritual teachings. The Dharma, for example, is a little like many colleges and universities—all kinds of interesting subjects are offered, and we can waste our time and energy trying to learn them all. One of the great masters once said that knowledge is like the stars at night—we cannot count such vastness. So it is better not to try to do everything at once, even spiritually.

At first it is important to concentrate on those teachings that are most immediately relevant to us—teachings for which we have the background. Otherwise we waste our time, and gain only frustration. Be content with proceeding gradually, step by step, keeping motivation strong and persevering in meditation practice. In developing meditation the slowest way is the fastest way. When we cultivate our meditation carefully, without forcing, the results will always be clear: although we may not sense each day's growth, the growth is steady. This path is not like pouring rain, which forces us to shelter, but more like snow gently blanketing the land.

Make your meditation casual, open—not self-conscious or forced. Then meditation experiences will come. Experiences in themselves are not so valuable, but they can be a form of extension to the meditation: certain experiences can touch the subtleties of the mind, and help to clarify the nature of existence.

Meditation is something you do for yourself—for your own balance and health. All I can do is direct, point, and give advice, challenging your assumptions or pointing out more productive ways to proceed. Once you have accurate instructions, once you understand the problems, doubts, and fixations that can be encountered, you need to investigate for yourself through daily meditation. Regularity is important: even if you can spend only thirty minutes each morning and evening, results will come. Begin by relaxing the body; let the breath settle into a natural rhythm, and allow the mind to become completely silent, free of thoughts and the need to respond to external distractions.

Motivation is also very important. As you meditate more, motivation becomes voluntary, but you can easily become sort of numb or dull, and even though you are sitting there you can become very bored. This is more reason to meditate very loosely, but at the same time very energetically. When you were younger, say fifteen or eighteen, you may have had many questions—"What is the meaning of life? Who am I?"—and you might have experienced a certain anxiety to find the answers. Later on you may have become more involved with work and personal relationships; after you have had many experiences, questions may return: "What am I doing here?" "Why and I doing these things?" Meanwhile you may have forgotten your original questions. Perhaps you have been involved in business or you have attempted to enjoy the many things life offers, or you have had much suffering. Perhaps your relationship fell apart; or you realize that there is no future in your job, and everything seems hopeless. Then ask yourself these questions again, because ultimately whatever you do in this life depends on you. Your best protector and your best friend is you yourself, your own meditation, your own inner health and growth, your own spiritual path.

So now the question comes, what is Buddhist philosophy, what is Buddhist teaching? What does meditation mean? The Buddha's teaching is a way of living, a lifestyle, learning how to deal with everyday situations and how to live and work in a practical and positive way. Even though you may not necessarily become enlightened in one day, the Buddha's teaching is not for later but for right now. Now be comfortable, now be positive, now fully enjoy whatever you are doing. Otherwise our life just goes up and down, and meanwhile we remain confused, engulfed in chaos and endless struggling. The teaching itself is a way of life, a pattern for living on a practical level without going to extremes. The Buddhadharma challenges us to change our patterns of suffering so we can find just what we need every moment.

It seems that meditation is the most effective method to overcome all suffering, agitation, anxiety, worry, and inner turmoil. If the mind becomes quieter and less confused by daily situations, then this in itself is something very significant, and you will most likely experience many more positive changes in the weeks, months, and years to follow.

Keep in mind that early teacher in Tibet, who said that the manifestations of knowledge are like the stars at night—there are so many that you cannot count them. So it is better to focus on the important ones—what is your life, what is the healthiest way to live—and develop your insights gradually, day by day. Right now, you may have many insights or ideals that you are not ready to accomplish, but if you progress gradually, step by step, your motivation will increase. Your inner confidence will become as indestructible as a diamond, and no one will be able to take it from you.

Once you begin to investigate, become more aware, and meditate with full and complete dedication, you will soon find that sustained efforts produce positive results: investigation brings clarity, awareness brings satisfaction, and meditation just naturally comes, like the morning sun. Everything begins to fall into place. Even discouragements lose their power to upset you.

When you nourish yourself in this way, you become your own teacher and no longer need to depend on others. I can point out certain things, or push you to examine yourself, or point out where the danger lies, but you must provide the effort. Even the Buddha himself said that he can only show you the map, but you yourself need to take the initiative. You should not think that there is an easy or magic way. If it does exist then you will have to find it on your own.

CHAPTER 2

ATTITUDES FOR MEDITATION

creating the right mindset

As long as we have a mind and body, our natural being is meditation. This is one of the most important truths we can discover about ourselves. In the beginning we can point this out using only words. But once we remove all our fixed patterns of perceiving and behaving, our natural being is immediately present. When bees extract the nectar from flowers they do not destroy the flower—the flower is there, and the bees leave it there. Similarly, we can leave behind our concepts, emotions, and ideas—especially ego and self-image—and use only their energy to become meditation.

In this chapter we explore all these themes, from finding confidence in ourselves through how to overcome anxiety and balance the emotions, to releasing ourselves from our self-image. In this way we can prepare our minds to touch the true experience of meditation that lies within us all.

FINDING SPIRITUAL CONFIDENCE

Spiritual confidence is more difficult to attain than worldly confidence. We can easily learn to drive a car, fix a lawnmower, or talk informatively on a variety of subjects. But how can we learn to attain inner confidence? There are no specific steps to follow. Yet, by utilizing the insight, strength, and confidence gained from meditation we naturally discover the truth that is always within us. And in becoming more confident of our experience, we come to see that devotional or sentimental beliefs are not so important. We learn to believe and trust in ourselves.

When we look at our ordinary experience with an attitude of openness, free from judgments or divisive concepts, we see "subject" and "object" naturally as one. In this way the spiritual path becomes a part of our lives—not just an abstract ideal reserved for special occasions. When meditative experience is truly a part of us, spiritual qualities naturally express themselves in our daily lives, and we can be confident that our meditative awareness will carry us through whatever situations we encounter.

Once this inspiration and self-confidence becomes our teacher, and once we contact this inner guide, we can always rely on our experience and realization, rather than on what is outside ourselves. Our daily lives give us the substance of our learning process. There is the raw material—our flesh, our breath, our environment. When we learn to accept and appreciate ourselves without selfishness or ego-grasping, instead of floundering in negativity and self-condemnation, we begin to evolve positive qualities— strength, confidence, and feelings of inner lightness.

Yet although the potential for enlightenment is always within us, most of us do not experience it. We are trapped by our dualistic minds. Cultures and religions tend to teach a dualistic view of

existence, and most of us have difficulties freeing ourselves from the rigid concepts of these systems. Because of our basic tendency to polarize experience, we forget to use our awareness in difficult situations. We become "attached" to a problem and let it control our minds, or we feel that we have to evaluate the situation. We waste time and energy. However, as our meditative experience deepens, we feel less need to discriminate and judge. We begin to transcend our dualistic tendencies by developing stability and balance, and by realizing that spiritual truth is found in ourselves and our daily lives.

We may have some idea that a place of ultimate understanding exists—but heaven is not necessarily somewhere else. It is within the nature of our minds, and this we reach through awareness and meditation. We just accept each situation as it comes, and follow our inner guidance—our intuition, our own hearts.

In order to improve our awareness, it is useful to examine our self-image and personality by asking ourselves, "Where am I? What am I doing?" This can help us stay "within" the state of meditation and can increase our attentiveness to the specific situations in which we find ourselves. It can bring us out of cloudy mental dialogues and image-building, and thus help us to live more full and meaningful lives.

To be sure that our meditation or awareness has a firm foundation, we can check it from time to time. When we are meditating in a very quiet setting, our minds may seem very positive, calm, and peaceful—but when we go out into the world, to our homes or offices, or when we encounter difficult or threatening situations, we may find that negative emotions can still overpower us. But rather than avoiding these situations or trying to hide from them, we can learn to welcome them and use them—for they can help us to test and strengthen the insight and the power of our meditation.

It is even possible to have peak experiences during moments of anxiety, anger, or resentment, for the basic energy is there, ready to be transformed. As the potential for realization is inherent within our minds, it is also within the emotions themselves. This potential is in every instant of our lives, and through meditation we can learn to reach it.

One helpful practice is to meditate equally on our positive and negative feelings—not holding to that which feels good, or avoiding that which is painful. In this way we can discover and use the positive qualities that exist even within the negativities of our minds. We then no longer feel the need to identify with or reject any of our emotions; we experience them directly, not discriminating between them. By developing and improving our awareness, we can transcend our negative emotions; they begin to lose their hold on us, and we start to feel lighter and more confident. Through these experiences we can even penetrate the nature of reality—and at these rare moments we can experience great joy.

When the world seems to be continually indulging itself in endless sensations and fascinations, we can protect ourselves and our integrity by firmly deciding to guide ourselves away from unwholesome or enmeshing influences. It is important to listen to our inner guidance rather than be swayed by others, for we can very easily drift away from even our strongest realizations and determinations for positive action. So we need to sustain our initial dedication to the truth, no matter what may occur— emotional storms or threatening situations. The person who is committed to truth and genuine understanding never gives up; this tenacity is one of the most important foundations for discovering reality.

Sometimes even intelligent people get caught in the pattern of mindlessly following others. If this happens to us, over a period of time we can lose our original self-confidence and balance, and we may even begin to feel like a failure. Once this weakness manifests, we become vulnerable to negative emotions and destructive situations, which pull us further off balance. It is like an infection that is extremely hard to cure. Our psychological conflicts become so entrenched that our minds spin endlessly in circles.

Once we reject our inner guidance, it is not easy to find it again, because our views and motivations may have changed. So, like a person groping in the dark who finds a sure guide, once we make contact with our strength and awareness, we should not let it go. This is important, because there are times when we feel weak or vulnerable. It is not always easy to have faith in our own judgment, but when we follow the truth as we understand it, we learn to be confident in ourselves and enjoy each moment. When we live our lives in this way, we can look back and realize how much we have learned and accomplished, and how fortunate we are to have gained so much understanding. Even now, we know enough to have confidence in ourselves—and this is a tremendous source of guidance and protection.

Each day we can expand our openness so that awareness flows freely and naturally. We do not need any other preparation. We may try to meditate for many years without success; but with this openness, in a very short time, we can learn to meditate perfectly with no trouble at all. When we meditate with such openness and leave all doubts and hesitations behind, our inner guidance automatically leads us to the teachings within. The more our awareness develops, the more we open to spontaneous mind experience.

One of my teachers once explained that great fighters, such as the samurai, perfect every move, every gesture before they engage in battle, so that when they encounter the enemy, they are completely prepared. They have no doubt about how to maneuver; they no longer even think about it. They just do it, and every move is automatically perfect.

Similarly, in meditation, until we have complete confidence in ourselves and there are no questions left to be asked, everything is practice and preparation. No matter what we are doing, we can practice staying in awareness, in the spontaneous, present moment. There is no need to ask, "How is it? What is it? Who is it?" We learn just to meditate perfectly without any restrictions or second thoughts.

We might ask, then, why we need preliminary physical and mental purification and why we need to learn specific techniques. These practices are needed because it is so difficult to directly penetrate the "secret path" of meditation. However, once we understand meditation, once we have the key, we can intuitively remain in that state of awareness no matter what we do.

When we have discovered for ourselves something of value, it will always stay with us; we will not get this certainty about its value from anyone else. So we should develop confidence and encourage ourselves, realizing that our lives are very precious and that our ordinary experience is the true path of knowledge. When we know that what we are doing is "right" and that we are attaining our goal, we stop depending upon others, and truly begin to appreciate our lives.

As we practice meditation and test our experience, we learn the true meaning of the saying, "Truth is like gold: the more it is burned and beaten, the finer its quality becomes." Once we go through a true process of self-discovery, no one can take away our self-confidence; the inspiration comes from within, and we know without needing to be told. In some ways this is the only teaching that makes sense, and it is always there for us to consult, because truth is transmitted through self-knowledge. So we can remind ourselves to remain confident—confident in our meditation, and confident in our experience.

LIVING A FULL LIFE

Impermanence is the essence of our human condition. It controls much more than just our lives; it holds sway over the entire cosmos—all the stars and planets, as well as our earthly environment. We can see the effects of impermanence by watching the rise and fall of nations, of our society, and even of the stock market. Impermanence permeates all existence. We can see the changes in our lives and the lives of our friends and families, but it seems that the most devastating change in human life—death—is always catching us by surprise.

In this society almost everyone is afraid of death—but to appreciate life fully, we have to face reality. Impermanence and death are integral parts of being alive; this realization can vibrate within us and wake us up; we see that although our lives are very dear to us, they do not last for ever. To be born a human being is a very rare privilege, and it is important that we appreciate our lives and take advantage of this opportunity for human existence.

With an understanding of impermanence, many aspects of life that we ordinarily find fascinating no longer seem so appealing. We become able to see through them and find that they are not actually that satisfying. We can then more easily let go of our attachments and fears, as well as our own little shell of protection. Thinking about the impermanence of life wakes us up; we realize that at this very moment we are actually alive!

We can begin by accepting each moment and enjoying it, but most of us do not know how. Enjoying life may be extremely important to us, yet too often when we experience pleasure our minds

32

project the satisfaction into the future, so our lives become filled with empty dreams that never materialize. It is difficult to truly accomplish anything in the present when our minds are always oriented toward some future goal.

This does not mean that we should avoid making intelligent plans for the future; it means only that we must live more fully in the present. When we endeavor to develop ourselves in the present, we will grow toward our future goals until they are accomplished. The present naturally leads us to the future, and the future changes according to how we live in the present. When we are confident in whatever we do, and all our actions are meaningful, then not only our daily lives, but our future lives as well, will be balanced and harmonious.

When we open ourselves to our present experience, we can realize that right now we can enjoy our lives, right now we have the opportunity! But much of the time, because our awareness of the present moment is dull or unclear, it seems that something is going on in the shadows, behind our consciousness, and we just drift and follow it. Meanwhile time and energy are lost and we may be unaware of what happened yesterday, this morning, or even this afternoon; we are unaware of much of what is happening in our lives. And when we think about it, we may find that we are basically unaware of how we became who we are today. When we were children we looked and talked in certain ways; how did we change? It is difficult to trace the transition. We can follow some of the experiences we have been through, but it is surprising how many things we do not remember—or we remember inaccurately—for it is like trying to recall last night's dream. And that is how we live our lives!

RELEASING FEAR, BEING HONEST

One thing we can be sure of in life is that we do not know everything. We have no certain knowledge of the past from which we came nor the future to which we are proceeding. We may not even know the present condition of our bodies, minds, and feelings. Because our understanding is so limited, we have to deal with an underlying anxiety—a suspicion that we are caught in our own ignorance. We may have a sense of a reality beyond the screen of our daily lives, but this truth is somehow hidden from us.

Our experience has given us some knowledge, yet, at the same time, we seldom honestly look at what we know. A particular action might be clearly advantageous, but often we choose to do the opposite, if it is easier or less demanding. And then we make excuses for our choice. Objections, opinions, and judgments occur in our minds to prevent us from positive action. Often when we attempt to do what is beneficial, we strengthen our insecurities by suggesting to ourselves that what we are doing is not right; we may criticize ourselves so continuously that eventually we retreat in the opposite direction, refusing to face ourselves.

So, two factors are present: one, that we do not know certain things; and the other, that we do know some things, but we do not want to admit to ourselves that we know them. Even when we actually see a situation clearly, we often try to interpret it to our advantage, and consequently we cheat ourselves. Our spiritual strength may not be powerful enough for us to actually face reality, so we forget what we know or refuse to look; we become lazy or turn our minds to other matters. We do this knowingly. So we find ourselves caught in these two destructive patterns: ignorance and avoidance.

The underlying cause of these patterns is fear, incessant fear caused by lack of inner strength. This fear divides our attention and motivation and thus interferes with our ability to see ourselves clearly. Fear is one of the ego's mightiest weapons for self-preservation, because once feelings of fear, inadequacy, and weakness occur, we do not want to face the reality of ourselves or our own lives.

We thus learn to hide our true thoughts and feelings so that the way we talk, look, think, feel, and act are not genuine. We cover up our feelings about ourselves and others, not wanting to realize that we are so far from genuine understanding. If anyone dared to suggest that our egos were playing games and that we were wasting our lives, we would find countless excuses to defend ourselves. But when we observe carefully, we have to admit that often we hide from ourselves. We may feel so threatened that we find it easier to constantly deny the need for change than to

actually change—even though underneath we realize what we need to do to make our lives meaningful and worthwhile, and how to go about it. Basically, we are just too weak to begin.

People everywhere in the world spend their lives dreaming of developing spiritually without ever doing much about it. But particularly in Western society, very strong will power is needed in order to develop internally. Consequently, although many of us try to discover truth, very few succeed.

This does not imply that spirituality has no power to help us, or that there is something wrong with the teachings or our ability to understand them. The problem is that maintaining a spiritual attitude is very different from our habitual way of thinking—and we find ourselves caught in conflict between the two. Our senses attract us to the worldly way, but our intellect and intuition urge us to follow a spiritual path, because it is ultimately more satisfying and meaningful. So we try to walk two paths that are in conflict with each other. Or we may proceed along a spiritual path for a while, but then run into difficulties. Our fantasies and expectations are not fulfilled, or we think we have learned enough and so we revert to our old way of life. There we may still find many of the problems and habits we thought were left behind. The difference between our expectations and experience can cause us to feel that the time we spent on a spiritual pursuit was wasted. Yet when we follow only a material path, we eventually experience a sort of spiritual hollowness, which we cannot ignore for ever.

Once we begin to change, it is difficult to return to our former way of life, even if we want to. Something awakens inside of us, and the positive force of change creates a momentum that impels us to continue. Then we discover that the spiritual path is right here,

EXERCISE I
LOOKING IN THE MIRROR

When you find yourself in a difficult or painful situation and can see no way out, a negative role may have you in its grip so that it seems completely real to you. If you suspect that this is so, try telling the story of your difficulties out loud to the image of yourself in a mirror. The practice will refine your sensitivity to your deeper motivations and self-images, and will help you to communicate clearly and honestly with both yourself and others.

1 Sit or stand comfortably in front of a full-length mirror. Be sure that you can see your whole body—you will be watching for your outward gestures as well as your inner feelings.

2 Begin to tell your story out loud to your mirror image. Be as full and as frank as you can—there is no one there to judge you (other than your own inner critic), and honesty is key.

3 As you speak carefully watch the mirror image of yourself. What gestures do you make? How do you hold or use your hands, legs, or feet? Do you begin to slouch, or move forward as your story unfolds? What expressions do you make as you speak? For example, do you frown or does your mouth tighten? Do your eyes open wide as if in disbelief or pain? Open your ears to your tone of voice. What inflections do you use? Is the tone animated or agitated in any way? Try to be observant without letting your observations affect the way you tell your story.

4 Be especially sensitive to the different layers of feelings beneath the gestures that you make. Awareness of these layers will bring you greater flexibility, allowing you to consciously shift your manifestation. Practice this exercise for five minutes each evening.

whatever we are doing; we may not have been able to walk the path deliberately, so the path came to us.

Even if we try not to believe that the continual round of desiring and grasping is destructive, our disappointments and frustrations will eventually sober us and help us face the realities of our lives. So, no matter what hardships or obstacles we have to face on the spiritual path, we should not give up—for if we do, we will just have to face the obstacles again later. Everything, ultimately, is our own decision; but if we vacillate back and forth, undecided, we are just wasting valuable time. We need to decide now to face our lives honestly.

We are constantly trying, either directly or indirectly, to protect our egos and self-images; this habit is one of the hardest to give up. We may wish there were a way to develop inwardly without hurting the ego, without analyzing, meditating, and persevering. We would all really love it if we did not have to work on ourselves. But unfortunately, without removing our obscurations and becoming clear-sighted, it is not easy to progress. Even when we think our minds are clear, they may actually be frantic, cloudy, or filled with feelings of "lostness." Sometimes it seems that we just do not want to see. If this is the way we are, how can we wake up?

We need tremendous courage to accept our pain and confusion, for all this time we have created and encouraged our suffering and at times we even like it! It seems we are not ready to walk away from suffering. We continue to make mistakes, create confusion, and accumulate frustration.

The ego plays many games with us and permeates all our feelings, sensations, and ideas; yet we are not even truly aware of how the ego creates these patterns in our lives or how our various negative attitudes and motivations develop. All we know is that we will continue to suffer from our pain and problems until we are exhausted.

We need to honestly observe our daily lives and directly confront our weaknesses and problems. Whether we call this a spiritual path or religion is not important; what matters is that our actions are straightforward and our minds are free from playing games. If we are honest and sincerely love the truth, we can revolutionize our lives. We do not need to blindly follow a particular system, but can develop in our own way by listening to our hearts and following the truths we discover in our own experiences. Totally committing ourselves to finding truth can be a positive and powerful step.

Regardless of our past, we can now make a choice for our future. If we are determined to work on ourselves honestly and intelligently, much worthwhile growth can take place. Honesty is required because we have to learn to take care of ourselves in the best possible way; intelligence is required because there are many obstacles to overcome. Unless we are relentlessly honest, ultimately we will cheat ourselves by trying to cover up our mistakes or trying to escape our difficulties, rather than confronting ourselves and bringing about meaningful change. If we want to attain inner peace and balance, we must begin with honesty.

The Monk's Fear

"There is a true story about a lama who was learning to be a practicing chod, a person who learns to conquer all fear. Chod training involves three or four months of practice, at the end of which a student goes alone to a cemetery every night for one week, and there performs a certain practice. The student carries a drum—called a damaru—a bell, and a horn made out of human bones which is used for calling demons. When the horn is blown, the student calls out to the demons, 'Come, eat my body!' The villagers are always frightened when they hear the horns blown. The cemetery to which this lama was sent was in a grassy valley, surrounded by high mountains. It was a windy, lonely place, empty except for outcroppings of barren rock and the screams of wild dogs.

Now this particular lama had been bragging about his powers. For three days he had gone on and on, telling how the demons had come to him, and how he had subdued them. He was a very proud man, but many respected him because he was a healer. On the last night of his week at the cemetery, a group of young lamas who did not like his bragging decided to watch and see exactly how he performed his practice.

Tibetan cemeteries are scary places. The bodies are put on rocks, tied to stakes, and left for the vultures, which leave only the hair and the bones. There is a foul stench.

The young lamas, hiding behind clusters of large rocks, saw the chod practitioner go to the center of the cemetery where he placed a pillow on a rock and sat down. After it had grown dark, the lama began to blow his horn and call out, 'All demons, come! All gods, come! Eat my arms and legs! I am ready to give all my body to you!' Loudly he called again and again, 'Demons, come to me now, eat my body!' He was praying extremely seriously and reciting mantras.

The young lamas put a sulphur paste on their faces and hands, so that they glowed. Then, whistling softly as they came, they crawled slowly toward the lama. At first he did

not notice: he was so busy blowing his horn and praying loudly. Then he saw the glowing faces in the grass, moving toward him from every direction. More and more loudly he rang his bell and beat his drum. Again he looked nervously around, and prayed faster and faster. But the glowing faces moved closer and closer.

Finally, he threw everything into the air, and holding the skirts of his robe, he ran off, dropping his damaru. The damaru broke and so did his bell.

The next day the lama's teachers asked as usual about his experience of the night before. They also asked where his beautiful damaru was that he prayed with in the morning. Every morning before he had told how he had conversed with demons and how cleverly he had subdued them. But this time he said nothing. He later gave up the chod practice entirely."

When we practice it sometimes seems that there are real demons and real fears. We can control them as simple mental events, but when frightening situations arise, it is harder to cope with fear. We may not be attacked by demons in physical form, but there are all kinds of different obstacles that can arise. Even though they have no substance, when we accept them as being real, we make them so.

As soon as we see problems arising, we can act; when we are always alert for obstacles, we can challenge them early and protect ourselves. Consider death. We do not like to even think about death, yet the time will come when we will be separated from our bodies, when we will find ourselves alone in our consciousness. At the end our lives will seem like one night's dream—a very long dream, with all kinds of experiences, but still only one night's dream.

TAKING RESPONSIBILITY

We all wish to be happy, to live full and worthwhile lives—yet life does not have much meaning if we wake up most mornings worried and anxious, and spend our days feeling frustrated or useless. We can perhaps find temporary relief in various forms of ego gratification, but eventually we realize that such pleasures are fleeting. If instead we learn to take responsibility for ourselves, and to live in balance and harmony, we will experience a deep sense of inner freedom, which will give purpose to our lives and sustain us through even the most difficult of situations.

When we carefully observe every aspect of our bodies, minds, and feelings, and everything that happens to us for just one day, we will be able to see and even to predict the patterns that will continue for the rest of our lives. In looking at the way our time is spent, we often find that because we do not schedule the things we want to accomplish, although the day seems busy, much of it is spent in confusion and daydreaming. We may even wander about, with nothing specific to do—no purpose and no plans.

Each day is a link in the chain that makes up our lives. So, on a practical level, we should always be aware of what we are doing, not in order to become rich and powerful, but to live in the most balanced way possible and to enjoy being alive.

We have a rare opportunity in this golden land to be self-sufficient, to be generous, and to burden no one. Taking care of ourselves is not so difficult when we have an open and willing attitude. If we were responsible for 200 or 300 people's needs, we might have problems; but it is not that difficult to take care of only one person. We weigh just 100 or 200 pounds and stand only five or six feet high, yet most of our problems are in our heads, which are only eight inches wide—and this we find hard to take care of!

Many of us did not learn how to be responsible when we were growing up, and the knowledge gained in ten or fifteen years of schooling often does not have much practical value. We find that as adults, we do not know how to lead balanced and meaningful

The Monkey King

"A monkey king looked down the walls of a canyon and saw the bright moon reflected in the water. 'Oh, what a beautiful jewel—I must have it!' he thought. When he told the other monkeys, they all said that it would be very hard to obtain; but the monkey king said, 'I have an idea: one monkey will hold onto a tree and everyone else will form a line, each one holding tightly to the tail of the monkey in front. We can lower our monkey chain down to the water and the last one will be able to reach the jewel.' So five hundred monkeys dangled down to the water, but the weight was too much for the one holding the tree, and all five hundred monkeys fell into the water and drowned."

Our minds are often like the monkey king—when we do not carefully consider our actions beforehand, we will be unable clearly to see the consequences, and our jewel-like fantasies, dreams, and selfish graspings will cause us trouble. When our actions are blind, with no practical or logical direction, we may get trapped in situations which are even more enmeshing than our present circumstances. Be aware of your body and senses. Come out of the fog of dreaming of the future or reliving past memories. Give up emotional romanticism and just be conscious of what is happening in your mind and in your feelings. Once you find your balance, you can maintain it, no matter what happens in your life.

lives. Even though we consider ourselves self-sufficient and responsible, unless we understand the hold the emotions and the ego have on us, we may only be deceiving ourselves. The moment we face a crisis, we learn whether or not our inner strength is sufficiently developed to carry us through our difficulties.

Sometimes we try to fight our problems indirectly, blaming others for our troubles. This leads to confusion and creates a thick, negative atmosphere within and around us. Although it is easy to criticize others, facing and overcoming our own weaknesses and mistakes is much more difficult. So, we tell ourselves that our problems will solve themselves if we can "just get away" for a while; or perhaps we think we can escape from our problems and the problems of others by following a spiritual path. But ultimately there is no way to escape taking responsibility for ourselves.

When we learn to deal directly with our complaints and difficulties, romanticized ideas about the spiritual path are no longer meaningful. We see that what is important is to always be aware of our thoughts, feelings, and actions. We can deal effectively with our problems, develop our potential, and discover meaning and value in our lives. This may sound simplistic, but it sometimes is helpful to just forget our problems for a short time. In the process we see that much of what we have been so caught up in has narrowed our perspective. Our worry, anxiety, and unhappiness have become obstacles to our inner balance and development and have prevented us from dealing constructively with our difficulties.

Emotional cycles and habit patterns are difficult to break, for our mental confusion often makes it hard to distinguish what is healthy from what is harmful. This is particularly evident where people live in crowded conditions and are exposed to diverse and

conflicting influences; the confusion and negativity can be over-whelming. People develop a sense of hopelessness—a feeling that there is no alternative, no way out. Eventually, such an attitude causes loss of vitality and total indifference.

Therefore, it is important to recognize the power of our emo-tions—and to take responsibility for them by creating a light and positive atmosphere around ourselves. This attitude of joy helps to alleviate states of hopelessness, loneliness, and despair. Our rela-tionships with others thus naturally improve, and little by little the whole of society becomes more positive and balanced.

In watching our emotions we see how they are contagious. When someone is laughing, we feel like laughing; when someone is crying, we too feel sad. The same is true when someone is depressed. Negativity is like an infectious disease—when one per-son is negative, then others also become agitated and negative.

So, let us take the time to develop awareness, to freshen our minds and our senses—for we cannot afford to waste time being sad, emotional, or confused. At this very moment we can begin to take responsibility for ourselves. These are not ideals or goals for some future time. We can start right now.

OPENING YOUR HEART

The basic teachings of the spiritual path arise from within our hearts. When our hearts become our teachers and give us confidence, spiritual nourishment flows through the heart center (see p.87) and releases healing energies. At that time other enjoyments and sensations seem, by comparison, like momentary flashes. So it is important to contact our hearts and listen to our inner silence.

Often, however, our study or meditation contacts our thoughts and feelings only superficially. We do not accept ourselves for what we are, but spend our lives dreaming and grasping for pleasures outside ourselves. These fantasies hypnotize us and prevent us from touching our innermost feelings—feelings that then become covered with layers of disappointment created by our unfulfilled expectations. Fantasizing thus creates a rift between our minds and bodies.

Life seems rather empty when our hearts are closed. We may read books, ask advice from friends and lovers, or seek refuge in material objects, yet we may still remain anxious and unfulfilled. Entertainments no longer give us much satisfaction, and we cannot find anything of beauty that does not somehow disappoint us; love is elusive, and nothing at all seems very meaningful or worthwhile. We simply flounder in our problems, looking for some method or technique that will relieve the tension and pressure of our insecurity and fear. In the end we may just privately cry.

There are rocks in the ocean that have been covered with water for thousands of years, yet inside they remain dry. Similarly, we may try to understand ourselves by immersing ourselves in various ideas and philosophies, but if our hearts are closed and cold, real meaning does not truly touch us. No matter where we are or what

EXERCISE 2

LISTENING TO THE TONES OF YOUR HEART

Occasionally, after an extended period of meditation, if you are very silent and alert, you may hear a beautiful, soft music in your body—a sort of silent music between the thoughts. Through meditation and your own sensitivity you can contact this silent inner music. By listening to the tones of the heart, in time, the heart center will open naturally—we can actually feel how open the heart is and how well we are communicating with it—and this is the beginning of the path of openness, compassion, and commitment. However, as you practice this exercise, remember that it is important not to strive to attain any particular experience—relax without distraction and without losing awareness.

1 Begin listening to your feelings and thoughts, and to your inner dialogue. Pay attention to all that is happening within you. At first you may feel dull and cold; your heart may be tight, and you may have difficulty feeling anything at all. But gently and skillfully listen to your feelings.

2 Now listen to your heart—literally the beating of your heart. Usually we are not even aware of how fast or slow our hearts are beating. As you listen you will find yourself becoming much more relaxed and joyful.

3 Listen still more carefully—sometimes you can even hear a sound within the silence. This is not the rushing sound that you sometimes hear when your body is releasing tension, but the sound of your thoughts speaking. When your senses are very quiet, and you are relaxed and concentrating, then it is possible to hear different tones, each tone having a specific vibration. For example, sometimes you can hear a high, shrill tone; sometimes a deep voice. To experience these you must develop your concentration and awareness until you are completely attentive and open.

we are doing, if we are not open, no one, not even the greatest teacher, can reach us.

Although we are adults there is something of the infant within each of us. That child wants to grow, to dance, to mature, but he lacks the proper nourishment. The only way he knows how to find satisfaction is through demanding and grasping.

Once we clearly recognize that our expectations lead only to disappointment and frustration, constant grasping no longer binds us, and we become more open to our experiences. We can find satisfaction anywhere—a simple walk may give more pleasure than any other entertainment. But until we open our hearts, there is little inspiration, inner light, or warmth to sustain us, for we constantly undermine ourselves. Ultimately no one can really help us unless we take the first step, listen to ourselves, encourage ourselves, and give ourselves confidence by taking refuge in our hearts.

Once our hearts are open, all existence appears naturally beautiful and harmonious. This is not just another fantasy—it is possible to see or feel this way, and this is the essence of the spiritual

teachings. The heart reveals all knowledge to us. Why the heart and not the mind? Because our egos control our heads, and our hearts are much more free.

When our hearts are open, no problem is too great. Even if we lose our possessions and our friends and are left alone with no one to support or guide us, we can find sustenance in our deepest feelings, in our inner silence. By utilizing our inner resources we can cope more easily with emotional and intellectual situations because we are no longer involved in the drama around us. Even if we have to face death, we can remain peaceful, calm, and balanced.

So we need to encourage our warm and positive feelings. This warmth is not a superficial or sentimental emotion—the kind that leads to imbalance and often creates "panic" instead of calm. It is a genuine openness, which is felt as a deep warmth in the center of the heart, which in turn is our inner sanctuary, our own home.

It is in the heart center that our inner nature grows to fullness. Once the heart center opens, all blockages dissolve, and a spirit or intuition spreads throughout our entire body so that our whole being comes alive. This "spirit" is sometimes spoken of as the essence of human energy or the essence of truth. But whatever it is called, unless we allow it to pervade us, our bodies may be active but our hearts remain closed. We are strangers to ourselves.

When we are able to integrate our minds with our hearts and our actions with our intuitions we can find genuine meaning in our lives. Our emotional problems automatically diminish and we discover inspiration, insight, motivation, and strength. We become naturally self-nourishing, self-motivating, and self-confident. So let us look at what is happening in our hearts. This is an essential preparation for experiencing the truth of our own lives.

AWAKENING COMPASSION

Soon after we are born we become very familiar with our own suffering and confusion. Yet even after many years, we find ourselves still unaware of other people's sufferings. And our ability to communicate, even with those closest to us, is limited. We find it difficult to understand them, and often they find it difficult to understand us. Although we live in close proximity to hundreds, or even thousands of people with whom we share so many basic human problems, still we do not show much concern for one another.

On the one hand we feel we need relationships with other people to bring us joy and friendship. But on the other hand, we set up a wall to protect ourselves from involvement and conflict, so that we seldom touch, trust, or truly share with each other. When we were younger, perhaps we tried to be more open with our feelings, but we were hurt and did not continue. Our egos were too vulnerable or our sympathy for others was not great enough, so eventually we became very isolated. And even now, we may have close friends or family, but if we are honest with ourselves, we see how lonely we are. We seldom open ourselves to anyone; and even when we do care for someone, often our caring comes from a sense of duty or from selfish expectations of reciprocation.

But whatever our pretense we can learn to care for this frightened and lonely person we may be. Caring for ourselves can be a tremendous source of protection against suffering and frustration. Self-confidence can help us apply our intelligence and knowledge to make our lives more balanced and harmonious. Through self-nurturing and development, we establish a friendship with ourselves; our hearts then open naturally, and compassion arises from within. As self-confidence and self-healing begin to develop, we start to show real kindness to ourselves and others.

Taking care of ourselves is not just another selfish act with a spiritual label. It is possible to give ourselves real warmth and sustenance without being motivated by self-love, because grasping for satisfaction is very different from learning to care for ourselves. Without compassion, thoughts and actions are based on desire for egotistical or selfish gratification. But genuine compassion, which is the antidote to ego, arises from a humble and fearless attitude of openness and generosity.

Compassion is the bridge, the spiritual foundation for peace, harmony, and balance. The ego is the obstacle—playing games, grasping, being clever and ingenious, the ego essentially runs our lives. The ego has so programmed us physically and mentally that only compassion can break the ego's hold on us and enable us to develop our full potential as human beings.

Compassion is a healthy psychological attitude, because it does not involve expectations or demands. Even if we are not able to accomplish very much on a physical level, at least we can have the desire to be a loving person with a compassionate heart—the wish to help others, spontaneously, with no reservations. This attitude automatically opens our hearts and develops our compassion. Then we can sincerely say to ourselves, "If there is any way I can learn to increase my compassion or understanding of humanity, then I wish to receive that teaching—whatever it is, wherever it exists—and take the responsibility to use that knowledge to help others."

As we develop compassion we begin to sacrifice and surrender our hearts. We do not even care if the other person acknowledges our attitude or our actions—he may not even be aware of them. As we lessen self-grasping, we have a deepened feeling of fulfillment and satisfaction that can expand and give our lives great meaning. What else in human existence has such value?

Compassion is felt in the center of the heart, and the source of compassion is our feelings, our living experience. Until the positive energy of compassion flows through our hearts, we accomplish little of real value. We may simply be occupying our minds with hollow words and images. We may master various sciences or philosophies, but without compassion, we are just empty scholars trapped in vicious circles of craving, grasping, and anxiety. There is little real meaning or satisfaction in our lives. But when our energy is awakened, relationships with others become healthy and effortless—we have no feeling of duty or obligation, because whatever we do feels naturally and spontaneously "right." Like the sun which emits countless rays, compassion is the source of all inner growth and positive action.

So, at this time, when man has the power to completely destroy the earth, it is especially important to develop whatever is beautiful, beneficial, and meaningful, and to practice compassion. In the beginning our compassion is like a candle—gradually we need to develop compassion as radiant as the sun. When compassion is as close as our breath, as alive as our blood, then we will understand how to live and work in the world effectively and to be of help to both ourselves and others.

We begin by touching our own essential natures, and then we open ourselves to friends, parents, and family. Eventually we expand this feeling and share it with every living being, extending this openness to all of nature—to mountains, water, wind, sun, and stars. When we feel open to all existence, our relationships naturally become harmonious. This compassion need not be manifested physically—it simply arises through accepting and expanding an open mental attitude. The power of compassion can totally transform both ourselves and others so that our lives become radiant and light.

So try to visualize all the beings in the world—particularly those who have problems or who are experiencing pain. Especially remember your parents and friends, whether they are still alive or not, and then all others. Free yourself from selfish motivations and transform your problems and emotions into deep compassion toward all beings and all things in nature, so that the entire universe is flooded with compassion. Let this compassion radiate outward from every part of your body, and let us together send our power and energy to all beings so that they may overcome their obstacles and become healthy and happy.

UNDERSTANDING SUFFERING

At least once a day it is helpful to think about the loneliness, confusion, suffering, and ignorance we all experience. This leads to the understanding of how all of these painful conditions—from birth to the present moment—came to be. Once we understand we naturally become more relaxed and open. Our problems do not seem so serious, and we are able to enjoy life and even laugh at ourselves, because we understand and appreciate our lives for what they are.

TRANSFORMING ANXIETY

Awareness is always accessible within ourselves, within our energy. But when we are distracted or emotionally entangled, we may have no idea what is actually happening in ourselves. Everything may seem dream-like, and we may find ourselves going from one conversation or activity to another, moody and anxious, or with a false sense of spontaneity and freedom. At other times we find ourselves thinking continually about the past or the future, or struggling with current "problems"—inadequacies, hesitations, self-deceptions, fears, infatuations, and guilts—our energies so caught up in a variety of emotional entanglements that we feel confused, worn out, and anxious. By working with these emotions in our meditation, we can learn to free ourselves from their influence.

One of the most difficult emotions to handle is anxiety. On the surface anxiety may not seem that great a problem, but as far as our human consciousness is concerned, it can disturb our meditative openness to the point where we completely lose our balance. We let positive opportunities slip away through loss of awareness; anxiety pushes and divides us, creating separateness, confusion, and dissatisfaction. And when we are not mindful of our anxiety it becomes increasingly hard to control.

Life is moving and changing much faster than even a few years ago. Many exciting and fascinating things are happening every day—it is all a beautiful dance, and every situation, every activity, and every thought has its place in our practice. Each experience can teach us how foolish it is to be so dramatic and serious—even our difficulties can be transcended, for nothing is permanent.

Yet at the same time this realization is not easy to put into practice. We are so tied up in negative patterns that we may even be strengthening our negative emotions without knowing we are doing so. When we are unaware, when we are sad, depressed, or unhappy, we are like bees trapped in a jar—they buzz around in restless patterns, with no way of escape. Yet we are not completely trapped. Our emotional problems and negative attitudes are in one way part of our learning process.

By means of awareness we can become sensitive to our emotions as they arise and thus begin to break our emotional patterns and our attachments to them. The more our awareness increases, the more time we have for positive action; three weeks for the person who is aware are the same as three months for the person who is not. When we remind ourselves to keep our bodies and minds in harmony with our awareness, we become familiar with every change in our thoughts and moods; and we can remember to bring our awareness immediately into the midst of any situation that could disturb our balance. This practice is like learning to swim; once we learn the first strokes, with practice we will gradually be able to swim—not just for five or ten minutes, but for as long as we like. Similarly, we can develop continuous meditation if we sustain an open attitude in whatever activities we are involved.

Because anxiety causes, consciously or unconsciously, many of our problems, it is important to deal with it as soon as it arises. The best antidote to anxiety is meditation. When we learn to control the emotions through meditation, we become less burdened by our problems; our bodies and minds become very still, and anxiety starts to dissolve in calm relaxation and quiet. We can then begin to work with our problems directly, for we no longer feel the need to escape them. Our tenseness and blockages naturally ease. Thus, we are no longer caught in a cycle of anxiety, and we can enjoy living in our bodies and minds. This is the first stage of meditation.

EXERCISE 3
BODY OF ENERGY

This exercise releases tension from the muscles of the lower abdomen, relieves emotions, and refreshes the whole body. Do the exercise three times (beginning with three slow rolls, then six to nine quick rolls), resting on your back for a few minutes after each repetition, and at the end of the whole series.

1   Lie on your back with your arms at your sides, and your legs separated about the width of your pelvis.

2   Bend your knees, one at a time, and place your feet on the floor. With the palms facing each other, slowly lift your arms to the ceiling.

3   In this position roll your pelvis and knees toward your chest, lifting your pelvis as high off the floor as possible. The back of your waistline will come off the floor, and your arms will move apart a little. Try to keep your toes pointing back rather than up, if you can.

Keeping your arms up, slowly roll back until your pelvis and feet rest on the floor, as for position 2. Breathe easily through both nose and mouth throughout the movement. Continue three times, expanding the sensations awakened by the roll. Now do the movement quickly, six to nine times, breathing gently through both nose and mouth as you do so.

Straighten your legs one at a time, lower your arms to your sides and rest on your back for a few minutes in position 1, continuing to amplify and extend the feelings in and around your body.

ACCEPTING CHANGE

From an ordinary point of view, the world of our experience is real. It certainly is not an illusion in the sense of a rabbit pulled out of a hat. But along with considering our world as real, we tend to consider much of our world, much of our experience, as permanent. Drawing on this assumption, we build an elaborate ordering of reality using the mutually agreed-upon sets of concepts that explain the nature of our world.

But in truth all the different aspects of existence are transitory, with each moment a change from the one before. There is nothing in our world that will last for very long. There is no reality to catch hold of, and whatever we try to hold on to will change.

As soon as an experience occurs, it is already past. However, we often only vaguely sense that this process of change is going on—many changes happen so slowly that they do not seem to happen at all. We often do not see the process, until suddenly we see the result. For example, when we look back upon our childhood, we find that we are not at all—physically or mentally—the same as we were then. Yet we still consider that child as being us.

In order to understand transitoriness more clearly, it is sometimes helpful to think of our lives as being like a dream. When we are dreaming, what we experience seems very real: we spend time with our friends, we hear music, we feel many wonderful sensations. Only when we wake up from the dream do we discover that the experience was not actually "real." The field of the mind has provided the stage for all the images, all the action, all the language of the dream. In much the same way, the waking mind supports and orders our passing thoughts, feelings, and perceptions. The results seem real and comprise what we know as ordinary experience. However, when we look back on our experience, we see that it is composed of nothing but transitory thoughts and impressions.

Actually realizing that all experience is transitory, that whatever we seek will elude us, can be very frightening, even threatening. Change is upsetting, and the idea of constant change is perhaps more disturbing than we care to think about. We want our world to be at least partially solid and stable, something we can depend upon. We do not see that if any part of our existence were

The Frog's World

"There is a story about a frog that lived in a small pond. Because he had never gone anywhere else, the frog thought his pond was the whole world. Then one day a tortoise came to the pond and told the frog that he had come from the ocean. But the frog had never heard of an ocean and wondered if it were like his pond. 'No,' said the tortoise. 'It is much bigger.' 'Three times bigger?' asked the frog. The tortoise kept trying to explain to the frog how big the ocean was, but the frog did not want to hear. Finally the frog fainted: it was so frightening even to try to think about such a place."

Like the frog we often limit our horizons by believing in only the things with which we are familiar. Although each belief system may express some aspect of truth, all belief systems are based on ordinary human consciousness and thus can point only to relative truths, never to anything more. As long as a belief system belongs to the realm of ideas and concepts, it limits us to a very small part of the knowledge that is actually available to us.

fixed or solid, it would actually pose a great obstacle. For change is what allows growth and development. Transitoriness is not a threat at all; it is instead the opening to new horizons.

Therefore, in order to discover all the possibilities before us, we must somehow learn to go "beyond" ordinary human consciousness, and enter the realm of direct experience. This is difficult to do because our minds know only how to follow ideas, instructions, and concepts; we therefore project the idea of going beyond, of transcending or transmuting. We are still caught up in the idea, and so we remain at our former level of consciousness. As long as we follow our thoughts in this way, we remain at the level of consciousness that is limited to concepts.

Through meditation we can obtain an understanding of the changing nature of all existence, and can then open to a new way of seeing. Inherent in the realization that our everyday world is actually always changing is the realization of intrinsic awareness. This awareness permeates all seemingly solid form. When we begin to open our perspective and develop this awareness, we discover a vast, unexplored world, a place where each moment brings a fresh kind of experience. Our dullness, confusion, and restlessness drop away with all other illusions, and our experience takes on new meaning. When we are able to see our world from the perspective of change, we become open to a new freedom and awareness.

Obstacles to our progress may still arise, but we can get around them; learning to "flow" with our experience gives us true stability and freedom. When we discover change as the real nature of existence, our old conception of the world seems dwarfed and limited. Our world comes alive; we are whole again. A new reality emerges from the old, like a phoenix out of a fire.

BALANCING YOUR EMOTIONS

A natural, vibrant response to life—engendering enthusiasm, joy, and vitality—depends upon inner balance. When we are balanced, positive qualities manifest spontaneously and we flow easily with whatever experience brings. But at times we lose our equilibrium and our perceptions become colored by emotion. The lucid and stimulating quality of happiness is clouded by anxiety and depression, and it is difficult to find fulfillment in anything we do.

If we suffer a serious physical injury, we are immediately advised to stay still, for moving about and becoming excited can make the injury worse. Similarly, in the midst of a problem, becoming emotional almost always makes it harder for us to find a solution. If we can stand back, however, and calmly observe every side of the situation, including the beginning of our emotional response, we will handle the problem more easily and also learn something of value for the future.

Nevertheless until we have gained experience with our emotional patterns, it may be difficult to catch an emotion before it dictates our response to a situation. Thus at first we know our emotions only by their results—angry replies, tears, or longing for a loved one. Yet as we become more familiar with our patterns, we learn to recognize the early signs of an emotional reaction: a tight, physical sensation of excitement in the abdomen, which slowly spreads into the chest, causing a dense feeling in the heart or at times in the throat. Unless we can catch the energy at some point during this process, it will be followed almost immediately by an emotional response.

If we can relax before the sensation changes to emotion, the tension in our hearts can loosen. One method of becoming calm is simply to be mindful of the present moment, without becoming anxious about the future, or preoccupied with the past. We can do this in any situation, just by being in that situation, allowing the experience to happen. But we must let go of expectations and concepts, or our emotions will gain control of our actions.

After an emotion has already surfaced, there are two ways to deal with it. One is to objectify the emotional response by blaming someone or something for the way you feel. This way reinforces and escalates negative feelings. The other choice is to go directly into the emotion, become it, discover it, feel it thoroughly, and calmly watch its nature. Rather than ask why, observe how the emotion arises. Instead of trying to push the emotion away, befriend it. If you watch carefully, without involvement, you will see this emotion manifest in both body and mind and then dissolve into pure energy.

Just by sitting quietly and watching our emotional state without attachment, we become tranquil. No other instruction is necessary. Agitated, restless feelings are like muddy water, which becomes still and transparently clear when left to stand. As our emotional reaction naturally subsides, mind and body become peaceful and balanced.

If we do not allow this change, we will see that we are holding the emotion fixed in the body, breath, and mind. Looking deeply into this emotional tension, we may discover a strange paradox: although we do not want to suffer, we seem unable to give up our unhappiness. We either cannot or will not change. We hold on to emotional responses, even the negative ones, because our emotional needs and attachments are strong; they form a major part of our identity. Letting go of them can be frightening and confusing; without these familiar feelings we may not be sure who we are.

EXERCISE 4
SELF-HEALING FOR THE EMOTIONS

When we feel that our emotions may be taking control of us, this simple self-healing exercise can help us to relax and to reach a state of mind in which we can merely observe our emotions and then let them go. In times of heightened emotional difficulties, practice this exercise each morning and evening for twenty minutes at a time.

1 Sit quietly and relax any tension in your body. Concentrating on the belly, exhale fully, relaxing the abdomen. Inhale; hold the breath in the gut. Still holding the breath, energize the gut, creating warmth there: make the belly area bigger, relaxing into the feeling that arises. Feel the energy; let your body be sensitive and relaxed, smooth and light like milk mixed with water. Hold to the point of discomfort, then slowly release.

2 Sit quietly, letting inner warmth rise from the belly to calm and relax your field of contemplation. Distribute this feeling throughout the body: into the cells, tissues, organs, and muscles; inside the tissues of the face and neck, the back, chest and arms, the hands and fingers, legs and feet. Even thoughts and images can be bathed in warm, gentle, calm, and relaxing feelings. Let this inner massage of feeling circulate throughout your body. During the day remember the warmth of that feeling and the joy that accompanies it. Repeat steps 1 and 2 three or nine times in all.

3 Concentrate lightly on your heart, and let the feeling of inner warmth generated from the belly relax and heal the heart with love and joy. Let go of any feelings of failure or guilt. Encourage awareness and give space to the full-bodied energy of cherishing what is positive. Allow yourself to appreciate your natural intelligence and caring, your strengths and abilities, and the value of all that you are doing.

Working with emotions can be difficult, and it is tempting to imagine that there is another place where problems don't exist. But this is your life—here and now. Once this moment's opportunity is gone, you can never get it back. If your precious energy is repeatedly spent on emotion and self-delusion, you will come to the end of life without realizing the deeper aspects of your experience. So whatever your situation and whatever your resources— body, mind, energy, awareness—use them fully right now, instead of wasting your time caught up in emotional turmoil.

The more you take responsibility for your feelings and emotions, and work with them—not just occasionally, but moment to moment, in all situations—the more balanced and healthy you will feel. Eventually, when an emotion arises it will last only a short time, and you will wake up almost immediately. You become like a dancer who has practiced for many years: although she may stumble and fall, she can regain her balance so quickly that every movement appears an integral part of the dance.

SEEING THROUGH
THE SELF-IMAGE

Our natural state of being is awareness: an awareness which is not of anything, but which is an all-encompassing state of pure experience. Within awareness our minds are balanced, light, free, and flexible. We are not, however, able to stay in this awareness, for our immediate inclination is to want to know who is experiencing what. As a result awareness gives way to our ordinary consciousness, which divides our perceptions into subject and object, creating as subject a "self-image," the "I."

However, what actually is this "I"? Can we actually find it anywhere in the mind? When we look carefully, we see that the "I" is simply an image which the mind has projected. This "I" has no reality in itself, yet we take it as real, and let it run our lives. The "I" then obscures our awareness and separates us from our experience by dividing it into subjective and objective poles.

Under the influence of the self-image, we perpetuate this subject–object orientation. As soon as we identify with our self-image, comparison begins; and grasping and selfishness rapidly follow. Then the mind makes discriminations and judgments, which cause conflicts. The self-image gives energy to these conflicts, and these conflicts in turn feed the self-image. The self-image thus perpetuates itself, tending to filter experience in ways that allow only its own rigid constructions the room to function. Neither open nor accepting, the self-image imprisons us in blockages and constrictions. Our natural flow of energy is interrupted, and the range of our responsiveness and the depth of our experience are limited.

To free ourselves from the interference of the self-image so that our natural balance can have room to function, we must first see that the self-image is not a genuine part of us, that we do not need it, and that, in fact, the self-image obscures our true being. The instant we stop serving the self-image and its needs, all our difficulties disappear, and our energy is released to flow smoothly. This energy can then be used to further enhance our understanding of ourselves. One way to do this is to step back and observe our thoughts whenever we are in the midst of emotional ferment. By going back into your emotions, and intentionally making them as vivid as you can, letting the sensations grow more and more intense, you can look at the grasping nature of the self-image: it is always making demands, always wanting more and more. By feeding the self-image, we perpetuate what we can never essentially satisfy. In the end we have difficulty finding any satisfaction, for the grasping turns satisfaction into frustration.

Frustration leads to negative feelings, but any negativity is in conflict with the inherent positive quality of mental energy. The transformation of negative feelings occurs naturally when we cultivate a positive and accepting attitude toward all experience. The resulting energy can make us more creative, more aware, more open to learning. This energy can counter the action of the self-image which feeds on negativity and redoubles its strength with each frustration it undergoes.

It is our choice: to follow the self-image, which makes us its prisoner; or to develop a positive attitude, which brings lightness, fullness, and wholeness. On the positive side, no expectations, no frustrations, no dominating self-image takes us away from the immediacy of our being. Obstacles and distractions no longer divide our feelings and our mind. We are balanced and experience ourselves complete, just as we are.

No matter what situation we find ourselves in, we can choose

EXERCISE 5
DEVELOPING FLEXIBLE THINKING

As soon as we know the self-image for what it is, we know that we can change, that we can develop flexibility in our attitudes without giving up anything. This change is possible because our consciousness is by its nature not fixed, but flexible. We can develop flexibility in the way that we think, and begin releasing ourselves from our self-image, by adopting new perspectives on our world. Gain skill in the following switching technique; it will teach you how to see what you are feeling now and how it was before, sometimes feeling the two different feelings simultaneously. This technique thus teaches acceptance, making it possible to have positive feelings about any experience that occurs.

1   Every time you feel unhappy, say "I am happy." Say it strongly to yourself, even if your feelings contradict you. Remember, it is your self-image that is unhappy, not you. It is possible to switch instantly to a happy, balanced attitude, and to stay there by believing it. There is this choice when you are open to a positive attitude. Your whole inner quality can change, even if the external conditions do not.

2   Another way to counter the self-image is to become immersed in the unhappiness, feel it and believe it, and then switch it swiftly, electrically, like a fish darting in water, to happiness. First, be the experience, completely accept it; then jump to the opposite extreme. How is it? It is possible to clearly see the differences between the positive and negative experience, and sometimes to experience both at the same time. By jumping mentally from positive to negative and then back again, it is possible to see that both are manifestations of awareness, and as such have a "neutral" energy that can be used in any way.

our mental environment; choosing balance will give out life a sense of purpose. Quite simply, the choice is ours; we have only to choose the way of freedom.

EXAMINING YOUR SELF-IMAGES

How can we lessen our involvement with our self-images and learn to become more flexible and open to experience? First we need to recognize these fantasies for what they are: images projected by the mind that have no reality in themselves. But, why do we listen to what they are telling us? It may be difficult at first to stop "listening" to thoughts and emotions that are so much a habit we may not see them clearly. It is as if we have a close friend whose advice we've been following for many years. Suddenly we are told that he has been lying to us all this time. In order to be convinced, we need to examine our friend's words and decide for ourselves.

So it is with our self-images. By examining them carefully, we can learn to understand their true worth. One way to do this is to look directly at a self-image during a strong emotional upset. As the emotions take shape, intensify them, letting them build up until they become very strong and powerful. Make them so vivid and alive you can almost see and touch them. Feel them as fully as you can. Then use this vital energy to arouse your awareness to separate you from your image-making: step back and look directly at the situation you have created. What do you see?

When you look at the image directly, it disperses, for it is empty, insubstantial. True, the feeling is there, but as soon as you have lost interest in sustaining the image of yourself, in feeding it energy, its holding power dissolves.

FINDING PATIENCE

Like spice in food, patience is the secret ingredient that makes life rich. Relaxed and allowing, this gentle friend gives us the time to appreciate experience, to deepen our involvement in all that we do. With patience we can face the future with assurance because, in the present, our senses are nourished. Even when obstacles cast a shadow on our path, we know they can be overcome through patience.

Without patience life is like tilling a field with no horse to pull the plow—the furrows are shallow and crooked, and the work is hard and frustrating. But with the strong, steady help of patience, we plow furrows that are straight and deep, and reap a rich harvest. Our experience flows smoothly, and our activities are purposeful.

Nowadays we seldom associate this idea of strength and reliability with patience. We may even consider patience a sign of passivity, weakness, or lack of intelligence. Because patience can seem slow or indirect to us, we may overlook its value, choosing instead an easier or faster course of action. Technology has quickened the pace of our lives, and impressed us with the idea that all tasks can be accomplished, all problems solved, with little or no exertion.

In our impatience we are like spoiled children who believe they will always get what they want when they want it. When we meet with obstacles or problems that cannot be readily overcome, we are surprised and easily defeated. As conflicts arise we may become lost in fantasies, instead of looking honestly at our situation and taking action to change it. Before long our unresolved problems are like insects annoying us to the point of deep aggravation.

Impatience has a rough and heavy quality that debilitates both body and mind. When we impatiently pursue a goal, our breathing is rapid and sharp, our movements are erratic, and our thoughts run out of control. Rushing here and there, we can make frequent mistakes. Finally, if we do not accomplish what we set out to do, we become burdened by anxiety and discouragement.

In this way our potential for intelligent, positive action is held in check. We find ourselves under the sway of self-doubt. Like a traitor to our efforts, impatience can persuade us to give up just as we near our goal. When this pattern of incompletion is continually repeated, we grow increasingly self-critical and come to believe that all we do will end in failure. This is the worst consequence of impatience, because once we lose hope, even the spiritual path cannot lead us anywhere. We can no longer appreciate the purpose of our practice; we have lost confidence in the value of our goal.

Patience is the best antidote for these difficulties. With its soft and accommodating energy, we can accept and work with our experience, rather than struggle against it. Then we can appreciate all our experience, whether positive or negative. Yet ironically, even when we recognize the need to develop patience, we may be too impatient to do so. Instead of cultivating patience, we fight our impatience each time it appears. If we see ourselves becoming anxious, we try to force ourselves to calm down.

But impatience and anxiety can be our most valuable teachers of the practice of patience. Listen carefully to anxiety, for it can be a valuable sign that you need to relax and loosen your expectations of yourself. Learn to recognize how impatience arises. Watch the constriction of your mental and physical energy, the sense of urgency imparted to your thoughts and actions; note how impatience encourages the view that life is hopeless. Instead of running after patience, relax and let it come to you. Loosen the tension in your body; open your concentration and allow your emotional energy to flow. Let the warm, soothing energy of patience arise within you and flow freely through your body.

Through patience difficulties can be used to our advantage. Patience is like a best friend; it is comfortable to be with, open-minded and allowing. We may be moody, changeable, or overly critical, but patience accepts these qualities and cares for us on a deeper level. The balanced energy of patience moves easily through the body, radiating a productive attitude from our hearts into our work, our relationships, and every aspect of our existence.

EXERCISE 6
CULTIVATING PATIENCE

When you feel yourself becoming impatient try these techniques.

1 Retreat to a cooler location, perhaps going for a walk in a high place where the air is clear. This environment can help you cultivate a peaceful and beautiful atmosphere within yourself.

2 Pick a color that you like, and let yourself enjoy its qualities. Then bring the color to your internal awareness and allow it to touch and heal the impatience you are feeling.

3 You can extend this exercise by concentrating on flowers, art, or other beautiful objects or images. Invite them into your awareness and feel their harmony and grace. Then let their forms transform the fragmented quality of impatience into the likeable and smooth energy of patience.

LETTING GO OF PAIN

There are two kinds of "giving up" or "letting go." There is giving up attachments, and there is giving up because of difficulties and disappointments. The person who has inner strength and openness does not "give up"—but gives up grasping and attachment, and consequently gains freedom and confidence. Because he has no attachment to being a certain way, but simply follows the truth within his heart, no obstacle or disappointment can overcome him. The person who gives up because he cannot control his life or manage for himself does not fully give up; he maintains a certain determination to continue on, but does not have the strength or courage to follow his inclinations—he just gives in to whatever is happening. As he is not able to give up his grasping and negative emotions, it is not clear to him which way is right and which way is wrong—so he suffers in indecision. Although he does not necessarily undergo physical pain, he undergoes psychological suffering—the pain of not being able to grasp what he desires. The craving for sensation dominates him, and he is divided within himself.

Suffering does not come only from physical pain—it can occur when certain inner attitudes are imbalanced or out of harmony. When we undergo great conflict or pressure, making even a simple decision can be very difficult. Our awareness can become so limited that we even experience "gaps" in our memory. Even when we manage to make a decision, we may suffer if we do not achieve all we hoped to accomplish. And when we succeed at something, we may become proud and attached to it, then suffer through our fear of losing it. Or perhaps we become very tense in attempting to reach some goal or in trying to materialize some hope or expectation. We feel frustrated because we never get enough of what we want, whether it be approval or love, attainment or success. No matter which way we turn, there is conflict and indecision; we are caught in between and do not know which way to go.

These uncertainties create continual disturbances within us, and our minds become like internal clocks on which the hands continually move around in circles without ever halting to point the time. Finally, we become incapable of making any decisions, going completely blank and having no specific thoughts or direction; we just become passive and uncaring, in a cycle of despair. And we can continue on and on in this way indefinitely.

Because our powers of self-observation are usually not well developed, we are often blind to our suffering. We have to be able to look inwardly to discover the subtleties of our present experience, and this we find difficult to do. Therefore, it is perhaps easier to learn from past experience, for although it is often difficult to learn from suffering at the time it occurs, when we re-enter our feelings of the past, we can sometimes see them with more clarity and detachment.

Most of us experience a great deal of suffering in our lives as we go through cycles of stress, dullness, and restlessness. We try to escape this suffering, but it always returns. Yet when we have the strength and courage to look deeply into ourselves, into our pain, we see a strange paradox. Even when we want to give up suffering, it seems that we are not ready—we hold tightly to it.

But eventually, as we become more familiar with our pain, we may decide that we do not want to suffer any more. At that point we let go of our suffering and wake up—there is an inward change, and we clearly see the foolishness of the countless self-tortures we have created. This inner change is the real learning process.

LETTING GO OF ATTACHMENTS

In our meditation we like to feel that we are doing something substantial, tasting a specific experience, such as beauty, joy, or calmness. This attachment to experience ties us to our ordinary consciousness. We need to get rid of this grasping—this collecting of experiences and commenting on them. We need to cut these subtle levels of attachment and go beyond the position we are taking—beyond the senses, beyond concepts, beyond meditation.

Until we develop non-attachment we will always have to struggle with our concepts, our doubts and emotions, with questions of whether we are meditating correctly, making progress, or attaining enlightenment. Yet enlightenment never comes because we hold on to our desires so tightly that our awareness is not free.

So, first it is important to penetrate our concentration and, as much as we can, to let go of even our very subtle mental attachments. When we experience awareness and let the natural energies of mind and body expand, then thoughts may appear—but they are part of awareness, so if we do not grasp them, they sparkle as they pass. We lose balance and awareness only when we become fascinated by these thoughts and grasp at them. Each time we reach out to a thought, we move farther away from awareness. It is like going out on the limb of a tree to reach an apple—when we go out too far, we lose our balance and fall.

So, whenever any thoughts or judgments occur, we can just let them go; we can let go of the meditator, the meditating, and any meditated "thing." As we allow the positive energy of this natural state of mind to flow freely, our body energies also begin to move freely. At this point it is easy to meditate because there is nothing to practice, nothing to accomplish—just the fullness of being. Our experience is our meditation and our meditation is our experience.

The Brothers and the Hot Rock

"Once there were two brothers. One was mean, but also very smart; the other was very stubborn and also very stupid. One day they were both running in a field. The mean brother decided to have some fun and said, 'You sit here in the valley and I will go into the hills and send you back a big present. It will make strange crackling and whistling noises, but you have to hold it until I get back.' So he climbed up a hill, found a large white rock, heated it until it was red hot, and then rolled it down the hill, yelling as he did so, 'Hey, Brother, here's your present. Catch it! Don't let go until I come back!'

The stupid brother was so anxious to get a present that he ran and caught the rock. The fur on the animal skin he was wearing crackled as it burned. The rock burned through the animal skin and then burned his own skin all over, but still the brother did not drop it. He thought the rock valuable. So he talked to the rock, saying, 'Whatever you do to me, I won't give you up until my brother comes.' And he stubbornly held on to it because he thought it was important to him."

We hold on to all that we love in the same way, even though it can be extremely frustrating and painful. We also hold on to our meditation, wanting to see colors and visions, have warm feelings and sensations, and experience the higher stages. Our minds still want to identify, capture, and manipulate experience so as to have something enjoyable to report back to ourselves. Yet once we let go of our attachment to senses and feelings, we can become the experience itself—and this is the real healing process, the real meditation.

Within awareness we can experience another realm, another kind of world. This is the beginning of the development of our "psychic" potentials, which are a natural part of our being. When we reach a certain openness, we may have unusual experiences that can frighten us if we do not know how to deal with them or how to go beyond them. It is possible to develop the potential for these experiences very quickly, particularly when we contact certain energies correctly. So it is important to act with great care and to stay aware and balanced. Otherwise we can be trapped in an experience or develop in an unhealthy direction.

At such times especially, it is important to have a teacher or a trusted friend who has experienced these levels and who can familiarize us with the path. There are certain instructions within the traditional literature that may be helpful, but each individual will have different experiences, and therefore the instructions will differ for each person. So we must be careful; we can become confused by our fantasies. If we want to "fly," a good teacher can show us the map so that we can land in the right place.

At times, even when our meditation is going well, we may begin to worry that because we are not having any "mystic" or "psychic" experiences, we are not making progress. But we need not worry, for these experiences are not very important, and actually may bring us trouble. Experiences that are beyond our usual comprehension may occur naturally to some highly accomplished meditators; even to us. But they do not necessarily indicate that we are "advanced" or "spiritually evolved." These experiences depend solely upon the qualities of our consciousness. Even when they occur naturally, if we become attached to them they can hinder genuine progress. We may not be willing to go beyond them. We may not even know we can.

The real test of our power and progress is our ability to transform our obstacles and emotions into positive experiences. As our daily lives become more balanced and negative emotions lose their power to distress us, the benefits and direct results of meditation begin to operate on very subtle levels. If we can handle our problems more easily, can balance our emotions and transform whatever is negative into what is positive and joyful, then we are truly getting results from our meditation.

Even though from time to time we are unable to contact meditative awareness, we will never lose it, for we can always reawaken our awareness by letting go of "subject" and "object" and by going into our inner silence. There, the deeper level of awareness develops naturally. When we experience these teachings so that we understand them within ourselves, and when we practice seriously and devotedly, then awareness is always available to us.

The more we develop this awareness, the more illuminating and alive it becomes for us. Thoughts no longer distract us; we can remain open, clear, and balanced. This penetrative, open quality is like the sunlight that shines forth in all directions. When we do not take positions, the door to enlightenment is completely open, and we understand quite naturally what is called "universal" mind, infinity, or genuine understanding.

So, once you understand even a little, keep going and your burdens will become lighter and easier, and you will become more confident and open. Then you, yourself, become the teachings, for the whole universe is the awareness of your own mind.

LETTING GO OF "I"

In pure awareness our meditation is like the open sky—like empty space. There is no subject and no object. When we concentrate on particular objects, we relate to space in a dualistic manner—we look at objects through the mental patterns we have evolved to judge and discriminate our version of reality. These mental patterns set up a variety of subject–object relationships. Craving, grasping, and anxiety then come into being and give birth to the ego.

Pure awareness exists in the very first moment before these initial patterns arise. For example, when we wake up in the morning our sight, hearing, and touch perceive our environment freshly and keenly. But then we make up "sense stories," like children's tales. Our awareness asks, "To whom do these senses belong?" and suddenly we think, "Who belongs to this 'I'? Who is seeing, hearing, and touching?" We do not recognize that this is all part of a natural, integrated process. Instead, we interfere and say, "I see; I taste; I feel," and subjective conceptualizing begins.

This is the very beginning of the ego. It starts with the establishment of the "I" or "self," which is not aware of its original state of being free from self; so with the ego comes separateness and dependency. Theoretically, this is how the ego develops. Practically speaking what is happening is that every past moment is constantly being reinforced in the present, so the ego develops very strong habit patterns. And it continues to divide and separate experience until it develops a particular view of the world. Our sense perceptions then conform to this view, so that when we look we no longer truly "see." We have difficulty getting back to pure awareness because we are controlled by our ideas, and the ideas create separateness. In other words "Who is doing?" The "doer-one" is "me," "I," "self." That self actually is a part of awareness, because it is manifested from within awareness. But we can no longer see the connection, so our interpretations and concepts produce a tight, limited mind.

It is not so easy to go beyond conceptualization and actually experience the non-discursive state. Mind or consciousness, is always relating to "me"—to a subjective point of view. When we are meditating consciously, we feel that the instruction is coming to "me" because "I" am the meditator, or that "I," the subject, am within the meditation. We have difficulty accepting the fact that the way to meditate is simply to "let go" of all preconceptions and expectations and to "just be."

Once we can do this, we will realize that meditation is simply living in the present, and not being concerned with past memories or future expectations. But we also need to be careful not to grasp at the present; we need to let go of any position, even the present position.

Wherever we are going, or whatever we are doing, when we cease grasping at our experience, we can develop our awareness, and unlock a vast storehouse of knowledge that will guide us spontaneously from then on. When we stop grasping at experience, we can transcend the ego, and experience meditative awareness, which has no position, no "belonging to" anyone or anything—neither to mind nor to consciousness. Awareness has no concepts and no instructions. It does not focus on any object. Within awareness we become free from even the "idea" of meditation.

TRANSCENDING
THE ILLUSION OF NOW

Much is said about the importance of living in the present, about the importance of "here and now." But is there actually any "now?" When we carefully look at just what "now" is, we may conclude that it does not exist. We may see that there is no "present."

At first this seems absurd: I have thoughts now, and they happen to me here. Whatever experience is happening is obviously happening now. I am here; you are there. I can talk to you; you can talk to me. There is no question that we both consider each other real. This is all very simple.

Yet the reality is different for each of us. From my point of view I see one thing, from yours you see another. From my viewpoint, I am the subject of the experience and you are the object. For you, of course, this is reversed.

Neither of us experiences exactly the same reality. Even if we attempt to duplicate, absolutely precisely, the circumstances of a specific experience, it would never be exactly the same. Even if we could "give" someone else our experience, the experience would not be the same for him, for he would see it from his own perspective. Our experiences, our realities, depend on our individual consciousness. And just how stable is that consciousness? Drugs, disease, fever, heat, fatigue, all can profoundly affect our minds. We can see dragons, or colored patterns, or the room moving. We know that these experiences are not real—but what is real?

Our sensations, perceptions, thoughts, recognitions, memories, experiences, feelings, concepts, emotions: all are formed into a pattern, just as the structure of a flower is a pattern. When we take a flower apart to see how it is made, it is no longer a flower. Similarly, when we separate our experience into its "parts," it is no longer the same experience.

Our ordinary experience falls into a dualistic pattern: we divide the world into the experiencer (I, the subject) and what is experienced (it, the object). As soon as we have a particular experience, the I (the subject) thinks about, or in some way considers, the experience (the object). But our thoughts are only reflections of the experience, they cannot be the experience itself. Rather than  being single "frames" of experience, our experiences are superimposed upon each other.

Separating experience will create only a confusion of layers and divisions. We may blame this confusion on the complexities of modern life. So we try to simplify our lives by giving up our responsibilities in order to live in the "present." But this living in the "present" still turns out to be a grasping at experience, still a subject examining an object.

Our very ideas about what it means to be in the present, or to be here "now," take root and entangle us with their complexities. Where is this mind, my mind in which I believe that the ideas and experiences occur? Thoughts exist; we have a sense of the present; we have consciousness. But when we try to pinpoint the actual experience we are having, we cannot find anything in our description of the experience that is actually real.

What we do find is never the actuality of experience, but only some set of concepts we have formed about our experience. When we try to live in the "present," we set out to go beyond concepts, beyond time, beyond our usual experiences, but all we do in our earnest anticipation is reinforce our dualistic mind.

So how is it possible to go beyond this surface, or relative realm, when even the desire to go beyond it turns out to prevent us from doing so? The first step is to realize that all things belonging to the relative realm, including language, ideas, and concepts, are forms like clouds in the sky. They look solid; they have different shapes; they move; yet they are not so different from the sky they float in. Similarly, we make forms out of our different experiences by means of our emotions, our images, and our concepts. We develop "story lines," which resemble the cloud dragons that writhe across the sky. We usually regard these "cloud" experiences as if they were real objects, separate from us. But when we understand that they are surface manifestations, we can relax and contact the subtle space beyond the "cloud-like" concepts and "cloud-like" emotions, the space where there is no duality of subject and object.

Only experience can take us beyond images, beyond concepts and words, beyond time. But this is not our usual idea of experience, it is pure awareness.

Meditation helps us to let our concepts and ideas yield to this open awareness. In meditation we make our closest contact with our experiential side, where enlightenment, higher consciousness, is found. When we pass directly into any moment, when we dissolve the forms or "clouds" of concepts and yield to pure experience, we discover our great resource, enlightened space. We can mine our experience to find this great treasure that lies within every thought.

Once this understanding arises, everything is a part of meditation. We are centered in the immediacy of experience, and yet still participating in its outward forms, using concepts, gestures, and so on, to manifest our inner experience. This understanding is true integration, a genuine connection of our whole being with the reality of experience—a connection with the "now" that is unlimited by time or space.

The Cowherd's Visualization

"Once there was a cowherd who had spent his whole life tending cows and knew only the ways of the animals in the fields, but wished to learn to meditate. One day his teacher, Nagarjuna, asked him how his meditation practice was progressing. The cowherd replied that whenever he tried to meditate, the faces of his cows kept entering his mind. Then Nagarjuna asked, 'Can you think even more vividly about what you see? Would you practice this visualization for six months?' The man said he would. Every day, for eight hours, the cowherd concentrated on visualizing a cow's face. After six months, the man's face became just like a cow's. He even grew horns! When Nagarjuna returned and told the cowherd that it was time to leave his cottage, the man replied that he could not, because his horns were too big to pass through the door. So Nagarjuna told him to meditate again, but to visualize a cow without horns. After a few days the horns disappeared, and the man was able to leave his cottage. At this point, Nagarjuna felt the cowherd was ready to receive the higher teachings."

This is the way of consciousness. It can create an illusion and turn the world into samsara. Yet the same consciousness can pierce the illusion and the world is realized as nirvana. The means for doing either lies within us; the choice is ours alone.

CHAPTER 3

APPROACHES TO MEDITATION

energizing body, breath & mind

Meditation begins by making everything tranquil, allowing body and mind to relax deeply, and nourishing ourselves with warmth and appreciation. If you can be very calm and still, attentive to the silence within your mind, this silence becomes your meditation. In this chapter we learn that to develop higher awareness we must integrate body, breath, and mind. It is useful to consider the body as the anchor for the senses and the mind; they are interrelated. When our bodies and minds become one, we can understand emptiness; we know satisfaction because our lives are balanced. The roots of our tension are cut; we become fulfilled. We call this chapter "approaches" to meditation because it offers some core practices to help you further your meditation experience. But in reality there are no specific methods by which to learn to meditate—meditation is already within us, part of us; you just have to listen.

THE SUBTLE BODY

Generally, we think of the body as only a physical entity made up of skin, bones, muscles, and internal organs; but these are themselves broken down successively into cells, molecules, and atoms. As we investigate the nature of the atom we find certain forces that hold the atom together. When we consider the body itself more closely, we can observe similar elusive forces or energy patterns.

Within the body, on a very fine, subtle level, each cell or atom has a kind of nuclear energy, which is identical with the energy in the field outside the body. Relatively speaking, we cannot say that the body is like "space," because our physical structure seems quite solid. But in the ultimate sense, the space outside the body and the space that the body occupies are not separate. This total space forms a natural unity, like water flowing into water.

At certain times when we are very relaxed, positive energies increase so that we can actually "feel" internal and external space become one, as though our bodies were dropping away—we lose the impression of solidity. The resultant feeling of oneness is very important, because when our bodies are completely loose and relaxed, the energy within our cells begins to flow smoothly and naturally throughout our whole system, without any manipulation or extra effort on our part. This energy manifests as balance, joy, or even love.

In developing relaxation we can concentrate on a particular feeling such as physical calmness—then gradually expand that feeling so that it extends outward and inward, beyond the physical body. We can concentrate on our body stillness alone or on our breath alone, or on the silencing of our thoughts. And as we expand this feeling of inner silence, we can feel the energy circulate through and beyond our physical bodies.

This energy has three elements which together form the basic "pattern" of our lives. Our attitudes and actions depend on how well these three are balanced; our health, happiness, and even the length of our lives, also depend on this balance.

The first element is the physical structure or "body pattern" through which energy flows. The second we call "breath"—but it is not just breath. It has a quality of motility; it is a moving, flowing sort of energy. The third element is the "subtle body energy," which is more elusive than breath. All three elements are inseparably linked to and cannot function without each other; yet each

YOUR ENERGY CENTERS

The "body pattern," "breath," and the "subtle body energy," interconnect with the four centers of the body—the head, throat, heart, and navel. "Body" is connected with the navel center, "breath" with the throat center, and "mind" with the head center. Body, breath, and mind all come together and are integrated in the heart.

Each of the centers functions on many levels. During times when our hearts are open and our minds are not simply involved in an intellectual process, our energy moves to deeper levels and slowly into intrinsic awareness—into a sate of equilibrium that is one of the highest of human experiences. This awareness is felt in the heart, as well as in the mind.

has its own specific characteristics and qualities. Together they create the basic structure of the physical body, combining in a complex, mysterious manner to create what we call life. In some ways they can be equated with the body, breath, and mind; but they are much more than what we usually understand by these terms.

The "body pattern," the physical structure through which energy flows, is more than just a "body." The mental energy of our attitudes and actions creates a certain "atmosphere," which accumulates around us on levels beyond our physical substance—this is sometimes called the "subtle" or "etheric" body. Even though it cannot ordinarily be seen, it is always a part of us.

"Breath" is much more than our usual concept of breathing; it is connected with other energies, and its quality changes depending on our emotional state. When we breathe too shallowly or too heavily, this affects the rest of our system; when we balance our breath (by balancing our emotions) the body and mind become balanced, too. Breath is like a bridge connecting body and mind.

The "subtle body energy" can be equated with mind, but not with mind as we know it. Usually the mind formulates experience into thoughts and concepts, into subject and object. But there is another way of experiencing that does not create this dualism. When the mind is balanced, there is no time, no consciousness, no awareness of; there is just a special energy that is always present.

Each center of the body is capable of vibrating with positive energy, such as kindness, love, and compassion. Each center is also capable of a very depressing and confusing restlessness or dullness.

When the three elements or energies move through the centers, certain conditions or attitudes are produced—physical sicknesses, mental blockages, emotional troubles, or feelings of lightness, radiance, and total openness. The basic patterns of our physical functioning both determine and are determined by how the energy flows through these very subtle centers. Whenever we are sick, unbalanced, or have negative feelings, these are always indicated by the pattern, the movement, and the essence of energy within the body. Therefore, in order to be healthy we should learn how to balance our body, breath, and mind.

We may balance and help to heal ourselves by concentrating on various parts of our bodies. These concentration practices are simple, but quite specific. When our bodies are not balanced or our physical energy is being blocked, when we are sick or afraid, it is helpful to concentrate on the stomach, at a point below the navel.

If we are feeling lonely—cut off from other people—or if we wish to develop compassion or joy we can concentrate on the heart center. In order to develop emotional balance or to over-come nervousness, cravings, or dissatisfactions, we need to concentrate on the throat center. And, as the centers are inter-related, the more we concentrate on the throat, the more the heart becomes balanced.

When our mental awareness or our consciousness is not strong or focused, when we feel dreamy, lost, or caught by our dualistic minds, we need to concentrate on the crown of the head or the point on the forehead between the eyes. If we wish to develop gen-erosity or lucidity, it is helpful to concentrate on the head center.

Since body, breath, and mind all become balanced at the heart center, it is there that we need to develop more openness. Basically, if the heart center becomes more open, it is very easy for the body and mind to function well together and to support and appreciate each other.

EXERCISE 7
BALANCING THE BODY

This exercise balances the body, as well as having the added benefit of stimulating energy in the toe, knee, thigh, and hip joints. Do the whole exercise barefoot.

1   Stand well-balanced with your hands on your hips, your feet a few inches apart, your back straight, and your chest high. Breathe gently through both nose and mouth.

2   Slowly lift your right heel so your right toes and your left foot carry your weight. Now in a slow, continuous motion, with both feet always in contact with the floor, lower your right heel to the floor and simultaneously lift your left heel. Continue in a slow, smooth rhythm, lifting the heel of one foot while lowering the heel of the other. Your weight and balance will be primarily on the toes and balls of the feet.

3   Notice the point at which you are standing on the toes of both feet, as one heel moves up and the other moves down. Intensify the "high" at this point by stretching up on the toes. Intensify the "low" as well: as your heel comes back to the floor, push the hip on that side of your body back and down, as if sitting in a low chair, bending both knees. Keep your back straight. Notice the change in feeling-tone as the vertical range of the movement increases.

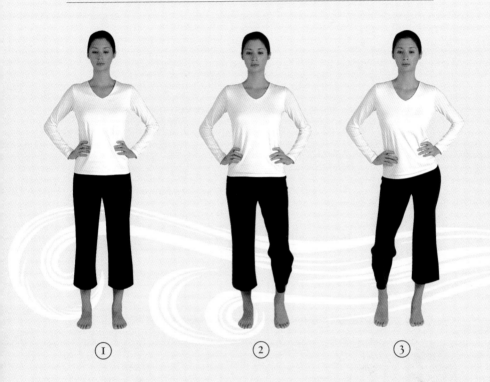

Continue this movement until it is no longer jerky or unbalanced, and both the breath and the movement are slow and smooth. Then (but not before) do the movement a little faster, but not so fast that you lose touch with the feeling-tone. Finally, slow down the movement until it stops.

Sit for five to ten minutes in the sitting posture (see following pages), expanding the sensations stimulated in your body, mind, and senses.

THE SEVEN GESTURES—
HOW TO SIT

An important element of any meditation practice is the posture used for sitting. In the Nyingma tradition, one fundamental sitting posture is known as the Seven Gestures. You will need a cushion (or a chair if you find it uncomfortable to sit on the floor).

The sitting posture itself is the first gesture. Take a comfortable, three-pointed posture in relation to the cushion and the floor. The buttocks form one point and the two legs form the other two points, making a triangle. You can sit crosslegged, or with one leg in front of the other. Each of the gestures could be seen as a kind of communication. This first gesture communicates our connection to the earth, our grounding in being and in experience. A feeling develops that expresses our connection to being: the beginning of meditative stability. The more we can open to this feeling, the more firmly grounded our meditation will be. What you may specifically feel is the bottom of the body opening: the genitals, the anus, or the place in between, which is called the perineum.

The second gesture is a straight back. This gesture can grow out of the openness of the first gesture, with the first point of contact being the perineum or the base of the spine. You may actually have the sense that the base of the spine is at the perineum. Later the starting point may shift; it may not be so well-determined or well-placed physically. Starting from the initial connection you feel at the base of the spine, develop the second gesture by straightening the back. This is a natural progression, an extension of the open grounding of the first gesture. The movement is a subtle one, but you may feel it between each of your vertebrae. Develop the straightness as fully as you can, without straining.

The third gesture is placing the hands on or near the knees, with the palms down—although this instruction actually focuses on the outcome of the gesture. If you see it more dynamically, the gesture unfolds through the upward movement that expands out from the perineum and onto the knees.

These first three gestures give us a physical base, as well as a grounding in feeling. You are forming a kind of pyramid: not a static form, but a gesture alive with communication.

In the fourth gesture bring the head back and up a little, without tilting it. Pull in the chin just a little, as though you were lifting the head and placing it on top of the spine. This may create a little tension, but at the same time the head can be buoyed up by the upward-rising feeling in the spine, as if it were floating on a column of energy. This can lead to a more natural balance.

The fifth gesture is soft eyes. Start with the forehead: let the tension you feel there sink into the eyes, and then let the eyes fall back into the head. They can be either closed or partly open. Usually the eyes strain toward the outside, but now they can rest in balance, equidistant between inner and outer, looking loosely in all directions.

The sixth gesture brings the tongue to the roof of the mouth, the tip lightly touching just behind the front teeth. This is a gesture of concentration and balance. The seventh gesture is to relax the mouth and jaw, mouth slightly open, so that you can breathe equally through nose and mouth. The breath, which is part of this gesture, may be the element that unifies all the others, or unity may be in the soft eyes, or the tip of the tongue.

THE POWER OF BREATH

The breath can be a powerful ally on the spiritual path, carrying knowledge, awareness, and nourishment throughout our body and mind. We live within the rhythm of breath, and by becoming attuned to its patterns, we find an avenue that leads directly to our inner nature. To appreciate the power and potential of breath, we must distinguish two types of breathing. The first is the outer breath, our physical respiration. As meditation practice develops, this breath grows soft and still, allowing us to recognize a second, more subtle breath. Smooth, silent, and full of feeling, this inner breath circulates throughout our entire being.

The inner breath effects powerful changes through its relation to the energy centers of the body. When energy flows well through these centers, we are in good health, both mentally and physically. The energy of the subtle breath restores balance, relieving tension and blockages while increasing the integration of body and mind.

Although the inner breath is a potent means of transformation, contacting it may be difficult at times. When we are excited or upset, our outer breath becomes rapid and heavy, and we cannot touch the subtle feelings within. Then it can be frustrating to try to breathe fully and deeply. This frustration, in turn, can stir up emotions and fill the mind with images and concepts, which lead us to become even more unbalanced.

Purposeless talking also prevents contact with the inner breath. As we engage in such talk, we stir up thoughts and emotions; we agree and disagree, forming opinions, and perhaps falling into arguments or negativity. These patterns of speculation and emotion sap the vitality of our inner breath, and leave us drained.

To develop awareness of the subtle breath, pay simple attention to your physical respiration. Notice when your breathing is slow and when it is fast. Cultivate a slow, steady rhythm; such even breathing in times of stress will stimulate a nourishing flow of inner breath. Be mindful, too, of how this gentle breathing affects your speech. Once you have developed an appreciation of inner breath, you will naturally speak less and with more meaning.

As our meditation deepens, the inner breath grows stronger and more pervasive. In deep meditation outer breathing becomes completely still, and only the smooth inner breath continues to function. Aware and light, this inner breath carries the vital quality of enlightenment to our whole being.

EXERCISE 8
FOCUSING ON THE BREATH

This exercise is a good way to begin noticing the patterns of your breath.

1   Sit on a cushion or in a chair, with your back straight but not stiff. Rest your hands on your knees, and tuck in your chin a little. Loosen your shoulders. Let the mouth fall open slightly, with your teeth a little parted. Relax the muscles of your upper jaw slightly, as if just beginning to smile. Relax any tension in or behind your eyes.

2   Lightly pay attention to the breath, breathing through both nose and mouth. This may be uncomfortable at first, but soon you will find it easier. Once you are comfortable, sense the flow of the breath as it moves out of the body and returns. Imagine that the breath goes out horizontally, like a river flowing slowly across a plain, and then comes back.

BREATH AND MANTRA

For many centuries mantras (sacred sounds) have been used in spiritual practice to focus and transform subtle energies. The practice of mantra enables us to restore a natural balance and harmony in our lives and to arrive at a quality of awareness that leads directly to the realization of enlightenment.

How do mantras work? Sound has a potent effect on our body and mind. It can soothe and please us, or have a disharmonious influence, producing a subtle feeling of irritation. Mantra is even more powerful than common sound: it is like a door that opens upon the depths of experience.

As mantras have no conceptual meaning, they do not evoke predetermined responses. When we chant a mantra, we are free to transcend habitual reflexes. The sound of mantra can still the mind and senses, relax the body, and connect us with a healing energy.

The healing energies awakened by the sound of mantra are inherent in the psyche. In the Buddhist tradition these positive forces are characterized as deities: each deity embodies a teaching, a quality of experience that is integral to enlightenment. The deities evoked by the mantra are not some type of personality, but manifestations of a natural bliss and transformative power that lies within body, breath, and mind.

Mantra practice is especially valuable to us today because it is simple and direct. All we need to do is relax as much as possible while rhythmically repeating the syllables of the mantra, either silently or aloud. If this is done with an open attitude and with confidence in the power of the mantra, chanting for just five to fifteen minutes a day will have a healing effect on the body and mind.

EXERCISE 9
CHANTING OM AH HUM

This exercise expands awareness and concentration. Breathe very softly through both nose and mouth, with your belly and chest relaxed. At the end of the exercise, sit for five to ten minutes, continuing to expand the sensations of energy both within and outside your body.

1 As you inhale inwardly chant OM, while also visualizing all knowledge being drawn into your body and mind. The entire universe gathers within the field of OM.

2 For the moment that the breath is retained in the body, silently say AH. This syllable transforms the energy of the universe into a still and open realm.

3 As you exhale silently chant HUM. With HUM the enlightened energy flows back into the universe, to spread its benefits in all directions.

4 In this way repeat OM AH HUM silently with each breath. Sometimes you can concentrate on the syllables, sometimes on the meaning, or on the feeling of the breath itself. Eventually these three will merge, and the practice will no longer be a reminder of our enlightenment nature, but an expression of enlightenment itself.

5 Try to practice this visualization as much as you can during the day; the more you do it, the greater the benefits will be. Wherever you are and no matter what you are doing, you can do this simple practice. Instead of distracting you, it will increase your awareness of the present moment. It can be especially effective when you are tense or agitated. Taking a few moments to breathe OM AH HUM will free the inner breath to soothe your tensions with its stimulating warmth.

The more you repeat a mantra, or maintain awareness of it, the more its power is activated. The special energy of the mantras given in the box on the opposite page is traditionally evoked through 100,000 or more repetitions over a period of months or years. When enough of the healing energy of the mantra has accumulated, it can be directed toward positive ends, such as curing illness. In Tibet mantras were commonly used for healing, most often in conjunction with other medical treatment, although there have been instances of people curing themselves of potentially fatal diseases through the use of mantra alone.

Even more important than the capability of mantra to heal the body is its power to heal the mind. Mantra can help us maintain awareness during our daily activities. When we are distracted by the demands of family, job, and personal pursuits, when we lose a sense of equilibrium and groundedness, mantra can remind us to keep our mind concentrated and attuned to the flow of experience. Chanting silently or aloud throughout the day creates a balanced perspective that readily dissolves confusion and uncertainty. Mantra also gently opens and transforms emotional states, helping us to deal with any situation clearly and directly.

All Dharma, or teaching, can be interpreted through mantra. It is said that when Shakyamuni Buddha taught, he uttered only the one syllable, "ah." From this syllable every listener understood the teachings perfectly in his own language, and in the manner most suitable for him. Through the power of mantra, all sounds gather into the enlightened field. The Sanskrit word *man* denotes the seed of the mind; *tra* means instrument for transmutation. Thus, mantra is like a wish-fulfilling gem that awakens the subtle energy of the liberated mind.

MANTRAS AND THEIR MEANINGS

The following mantras are especially effective for healing specific problems and nurturing our inner awareness.

TAD YATHA OM MUNI MUNI MAHA MUNI SHAKYAMUNI YE SOHA: The mantra of Shakyamuni Buddha transforms delusion and aids in self-healing. Visualizing or thinking of the Buddha while chanting can help release the mantra's beneficial power. This mantra is especially effective when chanted on the new moon and full moon days of each month.

OM AMITABHA HRI: The mantra of Amitabha, Buddha of the Western direction, inspires clarity and compassion.

OM MANI PADME HUM HRI: This mantra transforms negative emotions and suffering through the limitless compassion of the Bhodhisattva Avalokiteshvara. Like a sweet golden nectar, the sound of the mantra will ease the body and mind.

OM AH RA PA TSA NA DHI: This is the mantra of Manjushri; it embodies all wisdom. Sparkling with the light of clear vision, the sword of Manjushri cuts through delusion and ignorance.

OM AH HUM VAJRA GURU PADMA SIDDHI HUM: Guru Padmasambhava's mantra, an antidote for confusion and frustration, has a particularly powerful transformative effect in this age of turmoil. It is most effective when chanted early in the morning.

USING YOUR AWARENESS

Awareness generally means to be "aware of some thing"—to look at objects, to recognize, identify, and try to understand them. This is commonsense awareness. But as a living experience, natural awareness is simple and direct, open and responsive, without concepts, words, images, or interpretations. Awareness takes place within the first moment, not before and not after. It is immediate, spontaneous. There is no other "thing" to obscure the moment— there is no subject or object, no time or space. All that remains is within this openness, which neither words nor concepts can describe. There is complete freedom from our restless attempts to hold on to something, to be secure in some distraction or some trance-like fixation. There is no fear and no guilt—no desire to escape or be any other way. This awareness becomes complete self-acceptance and generates a fresh new outlook all of its own.

The experience of inner awareness is definitely not a memory or a projection. It is not like "this" and not like "that." It is free from associations with any "thing." It is a perfect, beautiful, immediate, and spontaneous presence. This natural awareness becomes its own experience, without tightly clinging to the past moment or trying to project the next moment—without, we might even say, any experience or any experiencer. It is totally free from fear, guilt, worry, expectations, projections, fixations, ideas, concepts, judgments, images, or any position whatsoever. When we experience this open nature, nothing is lacking, for any sense of "lacking" is simply the projection of our unawakened, ignorant mind. There is nothing to defend and nothing to do. The natural movement of awareness eliminates all obstacles to seeing things just as they are, and the natural expression of this awareness provides the perspective which makes all positive action possible.

At first we may be rigid, unwilling to let go of positions that feel secure, or afraid of falling into just one more answerless confusion. But the more we persevere in opening up and relaxing physical and mental tensions, the more we begin to discover a new openness and freedom. In this new process of exploration, old constrictions gradually evaporate; fears drop away, and a commitment to supporting this process begins to mature. How we accomplish this is very important, for the initial insight can easily fade away.

EXERCISE 10
WATCHING THE WATCHER

Whenever a thought arises, we usually feel the need to label and identify it. Try to stop this process. Although you can feel the thought, see it, and experience it happening, the thought itself is a projection of the "watcher." The thought is not separate from the "watcher." To understand this, simply watch the flow of mental images through your mind.

1 As past and future image-projections pass by, cut between them, not by looking at the thoughts and images, but by looking at "who" is watching the thoughts. Try to develop a feeling for the thoughts, watching the "watcher."

2 When you face the "watcher" directly, your awareness and the "watcher" become one. There is no self to watch anything. There is only watching, only the process. There is no subject and object. The process is the experience—or, you could say, pure awareness.

EXPERIENCING EXPERIENCE

We occasionally experience great joy, but only rarely. Because we usually feel unfulfilled, we tend to fall into the habit of day-dreaming about the future, or drifting back into the past. It is so pleasant to relive times when we were inspired by beauty, mountains, a river, or a forest. We long for similar experiences. In this way we feed our desire for positive experiences with hopes for the future and memories of the past.

In a sense all experience is available to us, yet we keep to a narrow path, moving forward to the future or backward to the past. With our minds caught in so narrow a pattern, we see very little of what is actually around us. Our experience flashes by. Our energy leaps from stimulus to stimulus, pulling our consciousness and awareness along with it. Finally every opportunity for a truly satisfying life has somehow disappeared.

One way to break this cycle is to make use of the very habits that established it. For example, we can use memories. Living in the past mostly reinforces these patterns, but at the same time, past experiences often gather deep and heartfelt feelings around them. By visualizing happy experiences, by raising and intensifying feelings such as love and joy, we can transform our negativities. The more deeply we feel our experience, the more we strengthen the positive nature of our lives.

We tend to carefully guard what little experience we have. We are closed and protective. As our experience becomes deeper, we no longer fear losing what we have, and thus no longer need to be defensive. When we overcome our fears, we open naturally to others. We develop trust.

As our experience opens to wider perspectives, our senses, our bodies, and our consciousness become vibrantly alive. Patterns of craving and frustration give way to the flowing interaction with the process of living. All imbalances drop away, and whatever satisfaction or healing we need is provided naturally. This protection, this balance, this genuine self-sufficiency allows us to open to the endless possibility of each moment and to discover the richness and depth of all experience.

EXERCISE II
SHIFTING PERCEPTION

Gaining new perspective by shifting our perception can help us to understand how our usual way of looking at experience distorts and limits our lives, cutting us off from direct contact with our surroundings and our possibilities.

1   Relax as fully as possible, and let your memories "float." Touch lightly on beautiful memories: green valleys, good friends, or happy times with your family. There are times you may remember from early childhood, wonderful times. Experience again your old room, your first friends, your parents when they were young.

2   Look at the images, taste the experience, deepen the feeling until you are enveloped in a warm richness of imagery.

3   Maintaining the image, imagine that it is in the present, and shift your feelings toward yourself. Shift them again away from you into the past, and then toward you, back and forth.

BECOMING MINDFUL

Constant awareness of whatever we are doing is even more important than formal meditation or practice, for when we are mindful every moment, our confidence and balance increase. And eventually we will understand how crucial every thought, word, and action is both for ourselves and for others.

As we extend this understanding into our daily lives, we can learn to sustain a quality of openness. When we remain open, alert, and mindful, our emotions and problems are not able to overpower us. We can allow them to arise without grasping at them and we no longer get caught in emotional thunderstorms.

Just as scientists test their theories in laboratories, we can test ourselves in daily life. When we are balanced and satisfied and find that our minds are clear and our hearts are open, then we know we are beginning to contact the truth within ourselves.

Sustaining our faith and trust is one of the most important parts of developing a spiritual life. Anyone can sustain an interest for a short period of time or even for a year or two, but the more complex and conflicting the world becomes, the more difficult it is to survive spiritually—to survive internally—because everything seems to lure us away from meditation and inner calm, from our sense of inner strength and wisdom. At times we may become discouraged with our meditation practice and think that we are just wasting our time and energy; that nothing is really happening and that we should just give it up. But it is important to be mindful of every action, in each situation, and encourage ourselves, for even one negative thought can reverse our direction. Each moment has the potential for enlightenment, but each moment also has the potential to be destructive.

EXERCISE 12
DEVELOPING MINDFULNESS

Keen mindfulness throughout daily activities—not just during periods of formal meditation—will help you develop your potential. You can learn from whatever is at hand. Whatever you do notice how you are; whatever you are experiencing contact your feelings, thoughts, and the quality of your inner environment. When you begin this practice, you will have to remind yourself to remain in touch with experience, and observation may have a strained quality. Try not to expect too much.

1   Set aside a few minutes several times each day to ask simply, "What's happening?" Then, as observation becomes easier, ask yourself this question more frequently. In time a lively engagement between body, mind, and awareness will manifest in every activity. Eventually observation becomes effortless, free from judgment, a gentle touch that does not disrupt the natural flow of the mind.

2   Choose a word that you use many times each day—a word like yes or hello—and, for a day or two, substitute an alternative word. Watch your reactions carefully. Do you become frustrated and give up? Do you become tense when you slip and use the usual word? Does a lapse evoke thoughts such as, "I am a failure; I'll never amount to anything"? Playful yet persistent self-observation, aided by such an exercise, can teach a great deal. You can begin to see how mind and body are connected: a change in one affects the other. Specific thoughts may be seen to be associated with particular bodily sensations and feelings. You might also recognize those circumstances that arouse emotions and cause you to behave in particular ways.

EXPANDING RELAXATION

Relaxation is a healing system that can be used to relieve our anxieties and frustrations—the pressures that so often cause our energies to stagnate, and thus prevent us from expanding our meditation and awareness. By deep relaxation we purify our inner energies. We can begin to relax by just becoming aware of whatever feelings we are experiencing—the tightness in our muscles, difficulties in breathing, or pressure in our heads. We need to be aware of, touch, and communicate with all the feelings that we experience in our daily lives. Then, through the use of massage and certain exercises, we can learn to loosen these physical and mental constrictions. When we learn to relax the body, breath, and mind, the body becomes healthy, the mind becomes clear, and our awareness becomes balanced.

Once we relax and our minds are free from distractions, we begin to feel more open and natural. This is the time to silence inner dialogue and conceptual thinking; once these are silenced, it is quite a simple matter to improve the quality of our meditation. Then, throughout the day, we can continue to nourish the feeling energy we have contacted, and thus continue to develop a watchful, positive awareness.

In this way we can learn how to expand awareness. First, on the physical level, through massage and physical exercises; second, on the mental level, through breathing and experiencing these feelings more deeply; and third, on the level of subtle awareness, through direct experience. When we taste that feeling, we find that the feeling itself has become infinite!

Thus, whenever we have a good feeling, we should expand it; the quality of that feeling should not be lost, for joy, love, and beauty are very satisfying and fulfilling. For example, we have

beautiful feelings when we think about making love; if we expand that feeling and touch it deeply, then it will last a longer time. Usually when we feel happy and joyful, and experience pleasant sensations, we try to preserve the feeling by grasping the thought. Yet this greater, expanded feeling is much vaster than thought, and thus we limit it by trying to encompass it by thoughts.

In the beginning physical contact—as through massage— is important, but later on the physical body becomes almost symbolic, for the feeling experience continues to expand beyond the body. If we can retain that experience, then we know that it is not just imagination—the experience is actually happening! This is a more subtle level of higher awareness which has an ecstatic quality—there is not that much feeling, only awareness. Later on we can integrate that feeling or awareness within the physical body. But again, the feeling experience is not just physical—it becomes a totally encompassing experience. Once the body is very quiet and restful, we can discover experiences and understandings that we could hardly have conceived of before—without words, without concepts—similar to pure knowledge.

On this higher level of awareness, beautiful feelings, like an inner massage, duplicate themselves spontaneously, like ocean waves rising and falling. When we find this place in our practice, we can exercise and stretch this feeling. This feeling of expansion is much more powerful than the physical sensation of joy—it is deep, vast, infinite. Our bodies and breath may feel very small, but our minds experience—without words or concepts—many different tones and qualities, beautiful images, and even deeper subtleties. The first kind of joy which arises is innocent, like a child's joy. It expands to feelings of happiness, then various physical and mental sensations arise, and later it becomes almost overwhelming.

As we develop this beautiful, balanced experience, we may find that it is quite close to what is sometimes called "mystic experience." It is difficult to tell whether this energy is "physical" or "mental," but all living organisms share this characteristic patterning—this pure energy. It is always there, even though we commonly do not know how to contact it. Often we need certain conditions—a quiet place, a light diet, or psychological exercises—to contact this energy. But once we taste this experience and feel it directly, we can bring that memory back into awareness and find that pure energy, or pure knowledge, everywhere.

EXERCISE 13

BECOMING AWARE OF BODY,
BREATH, AND MIND

We all have within us the resources to be healthy and balanced; it is simply a matter of utilizing our energies properly. The natural process of the body re-energizing itself begins to function when we learn to utilize certain ways of breathing, feeling, and thinking to adjust our inner balance and allow our energies to flow more freely.

1 Sit back, breathe deeply about ten or fifteen times, and slowly and completely relax your whole body. Relax your eyes, and let your mouth fall open. Follow your breath down your arms, your legs. Completely let yourself go. Give yourself time, and sense your entire body from your toes to the top of your head. Can you feel your heartbeat? Can you feel the pulse in your toes? Then, by running your hands over them, very gently and very slowly massage your head, neck, chest, arms, legs, and feet—so that you feel a warm flow of energy in each cell.

2 Now relax your breath so that your breathing is calm, and unself-conscious. Take a few deep breaths—inhale very slowly and deeply, then hold the breath for just a moment, completely silent. Exhale very quietly and softly through your mouth and nose equally. Feel the energy circulate through your bloodstream and very gently watch your feelings.

3 Finally, relax your mind. Usually, because our inner dialogues are constantly projecting interpretations, concepts, and judgments, the mind is very restless and nervous. Watch these movements of your mind, without following any particular thought, or performing any specific action. Do not try to concentrate too hard. Awareness is already there, but it does not stay in any particular place; awareness does not cling to any "thing." So just experience the immediate feeling.

EXERCISE 14
AWARENESS OF THE SENSES

This exercise expands awareness and concentration. Breathe softly through nose and mouth. At the end of the exercise sit in the sitting posture for five to ten minutes, breathing gently and evenly. Allow your sensations to be distributed throughout your body and to expand beyond your body to the surrounding universe.

1   Stand well-balanced with your feet a comfortable distance apart, back straight, and arms relaxed at your sides. Turn your hands inward until the palms face out to the sides, and stick out your thumbs so they also point outward. With your hands in this position, slowly lift your arms to shoulder height. Breathe easily through both nose and mouth, and try to keep your belly relaxed.

2   Now, keeping your arms straight but relaxed, very slowly begin to move one arm up and the other arm down. Move them just a short distance at first, concentrating on the feelings in and around them as they move slowly through space.

3   Gradually, as your feelings expand, extend the range of movement in your arms until they are both moving up and down as far as they will go. Expand fully the special qualities of feeling stimulated by this movement, keeping your belly relaxed and your breathing soft, even, and slow.

4   Continue for three to five minutes, then slowly decrease the range of the movement until your arms are outstretched in front of you at shoulder height. Slowly lower your arms to your sides, relax your hands, and stand quietly for a few minutes, expanding the feelings generated by this movement.

USING YOUR SENSES

Instead of having confidence within ourselves, we constantly look outside ourselves for approval and fulfillment. Even when we are continually disappointed, we keep on searching for and grasping after happiness. We entertain ourselves with parties, drinking, sex, coffee, cigarettes, or whatever else apparently gives us pleasure, but these pleasures are only temporarily satisfying, like trying to live on spun sugar. Such external pleasures can lead only to an endless cycle of wanting. They are really like poison oak; when we scratch, we relieve the itching sensation temporarily, but the poison ends up spreading over our entire body.

Genuine satisfaction is found only within our hearts, wherein lie peace and a subtle, ecstatic beauty. There, by integrating our body, mind, and senses, we can establish an inner balance and harmony. This inner balance then stays with us in everything we do.

Our problems are in our heads and hearts, and the solutions to our problems are there as well. Our problems arise because we do not let our hearts and heads work well together—it is as if they live in two different worlds—they do not communicate with each other, or meet each other's needs. And when the body and the mind are not sensitive to each other, there can be no real basis for satisfaction.

The bridge between body and mind is provided by the senses, some of which are related more closely to the body, some more closely to the mind. Because of this overlap, the senses have the potential to help the body and mind work together naturally. First, however, we must acknowledge our senses and experience them more deeply. The exercise opposite will help you.

EXERCISE 15
OPENING TO FEELING

Our bodies and minds are the foundations of meditation. Breath, which is like a coordinator of body and mind, is the essence of being that integrates them. Remain in the space, within the awareness, for as long as you like—you do not focus or hold your attention on anything.

1 Feel your entire physical body. Allow your breathing to become relaxed and quiet. When your body and breath become still, you may feel a light sensation, almost like flying, which carries with it a fresh, alive quality.

2 Open all your cells, even all the molecules that make up your body, unfolding them like petals. Hold nothing back: open more than your heart; open your entire body, every atom of it. Then a beautiful experience can arise that has a quality you can come back to again and again, a quality that will heal and sustain you.

3 Once you touch your inner nature in this way, everything becomes silent. Your body and mind merge in pure energy; you become truly integrated. Tremendous benefits flow from that unity, including great joy and sensitivity. The energy flowing from this openness heals and nourishes the senses: they fill with sensation, opening like flowers.

The external pleasures we thought would cultivate our senses have actually dulled them because we have not made full use of them. We usually pass from one experience to another before we know what we are feeling; we are barely able to sense what we experience. We do not give our senses time to develop an experience, or allow our minds and bodies to integrate our feelings.

Our senses are filters through which we perceive our world; when they are dulled, we cannot experience the richness of life, or approach true happiness. In order to touch our senses, we have to contact the feelings of our experience. We need to slow down, to hear and feel the tones and vibrations our feelings are trying to communicate to us; then we can learn how to touch—roughly touch, gently touch. Each sense has physical qualities, but we are often not fully aware of them.

Our senses are nourished when we become quiet, open, and relaxed. We can experience each sense, savoring its essence. To do this, touch on one aspect of the senses, and then allow the feeling to go farther. As we go to an even deeper level, we can intensify and enjoy the values and the satisfaction to be found there. As

ENCOURAGING OPENNESS

We can encourage openness and relaxation by visualizing vast, open space, by thinking of all external objects as well as our bodies as being part of this space, all within the immediate moment. Finally, no barriers remain. What is left is a higher awareness, alive and healing, giving warmth and nourishment.

different organisms have different structures, so too do the senses. There are various layers in our experience of them; layers to be revealed when we are relaxed, unhurried, and attentive.

Meditation, which encourages us to develop a listening, alive quality, provides us with a way to explore these layers. Using the tools of mindfulness (see p.104) and concentration, we can learn to root out tension and let our energy flow through the whole body. Genuine relaxation is more than having a good time, or resting; it means going beyond the physical form and opening all the senses. To experience this is to take a refreshing shower within our heart.

When our minds and bodies become one, we can understand silence and emptiness; we know satisfaction because our lives are balanced. The roots of our tension are cut, so our inner conflict ceases; we become very peaceful and fulfilled.

The more we explore the intensifying of the senses, the more we find a great depth within our feelings. Sensations become richer, textured with subtle nuances, more deeply joyful. We do not have to learn exotic techniques to enrich our lives. Once we contact this heightened feeling within ourselves, it carries us through our daily lives—walking, working, doing any activity. Daily practice means only that we keep on making an effort to develop our inner balance as much as we can, wherever we are and whatever we are doing.

Gradually we incorporate this feeling into our thoughts and awareness. It is a kind of spice that gives our lives flavor. Our mind, body, and senses become very alive, as if they possessed a natural intelligence of their own. Even physiological changes can take place. So enjoy this aliveness in which every moment is like a new birth; appreciate it and have confidence.

USING YOUR DREAMS

Dreams are a reservoir of knowledge and experience, yet they are often overlooked as a vehicle for exploring reality. In the dream state our bodies are at rest, yet we are able to see and hear, move about, and are even able to learn. When we make good use of the dream state, it is almost as if our lives were doubled.

In early childhood "dreamlike" images are a natural part of our lives: we do not force clear distinctions between our dreams and the solid-seeming objects of our waking perceptions. But gradually, as we learn the symbols with which to label our experience, we find that we run into difficulties if we do not follow the conventional ways of looking at experience. We tighten up physically and mentally. More and more, after our first years of life, interpretation shapes our ways of thinking, both awake and dreaming. We dismiss the dream state as irrelevant to our reality, so in the morning we remember hardly anything of the night before. We gradually lose our sensitivity to the dream state, and then we remember only very special parts of our dreams; most of them are forgotten.

Our ordinary tools of consciousness cannot cut through these obscurations because we cling so tightly to the surface of our experience. We can, however, use the dream state. Although in many  ways the dream state is quite similar to the waking state, it is much more flexible. In dreams we can manipulate images with ease, and by changing dream situations we can change our waking reality. Dreams are not fixed patterns of images or collections of reflected images; they are a direct channel to our awareness.

EXERCISE 16

VISUALIZING THE DREAM LOTUS

Practicing certain visualizations just before going to sleep can help us to attune ourselves to the source of knowledge that lies within our dreams.

1 Before you sleep, relax your head and eyes, your neck muscles and back, and finally your whole body. Clearing your mind as much as possible, simply lie there and breathe very slowly and softly.

2 When you are feeling calm and peaceful, visualize a beautiful, soft lotus flower in your throat. The lotus has light-pink petals, curling slightly inward. In the center of this lotus there is a luminous red-orange flame that is light at the edges, shading to darker at the center. Looking softly, concentrate on the top of the flame. Visualize it for as long as possible.

3 Hold the image. See how thoughts arise and the visual image of the lotus intertwines with them. Observe how these thoughts and images reflect their past and present associations and their future projections. Watch this process, but concentrate on the lotus, keeping your visualization clear. Other images may come into your mind, but as long as the thread of the visualization remains intact, it will carry over into the dream.

4 At first when you pass into the dream state and images arise, you may not remember where they came from. However, your awareness will develop until you are able to see that you are dreaming. When you watch careful-ly you will see the whole creation and evolution of the dream. The dream images, which at first are fuzzy and diffused, will become clear and encompassing. This clear awareness is like having a special organ of con-sciousness, which can enable us to see from the dream to the waking state. Through this practice we can see another dimension of experience, and have access to another way of knowing how experience arises.

INTRODUCING THE MIND

Until we are able to actually understand our minds, we remain strangers to ourselves, unconscious of our true potential. We may spend many years attempting to learn the nature of the mind, but in fact, whatever we experience is the mind. This does not mean that external objects are our minds, but rather that our projections of experience themselves are a part of the mind.

If I were to go back to Tibet and someone were to ask me, "What is American culture like, can you tell me?" I could not do so in just a few words. Similarly, there are many different ways to explain mind, for mind is experienced differently by various individuals, and there are countless types, degrees, and levels of mind for us to consider.

The mind is very versatile, like an artist—creating confusion, delusion, and suffering, as well as great order and surpassing beauty. It projects all form and supports all our inner dramas; it can manifest absolute truth as well as all our thoughts and emotions. Mind is not one thing, or many things, or anything in itself. We may use various words to describe the scope of the mind and to discuss its apparent functioning; sometimes we may label mind "consciousness" and sometimes "awareness," but the more we investigate and observe, the more complex the mind appears to be.

Most interpretations of the mind are limited because they relate mind to some other concept—mind is like this, consciousness is like that. In dealing with the mind, our egos categorize our experience of the world into specific forms, structures, and outlines. These become strict patterns, which govern our existence, like the constitution governs the country. They are, however, superimposed upon the mind; they are not the mind itself.

Because there is little specific data on the inner workings of the mind, it is difficult to discover much accurate knowledge about the mind. We may look at mind in its physical sense as related only to the brain and to a series of neurological patterns. Or, intellectually, we may be interested in how perception functions through the physical senses, or how we formulate concepts or make decisions. As we investigate mind from a meditative point of view, we see that mind is much more than the brain or a filter for perceptions, much more than just a collection of concepts. Through meditation we can go beyond meanings and categories into direct experience of the inner levels of mind. We can experience the mind as alive, sensitive, and brilliant—like radiant sunlight.

Consciousness, or simple awareness, deals with sensations, perceptions, images, and emotions, but these are just fragments, which, added together, do not make up the whole mind. Mind is far vaster than all these things put together. Buddhist psychology posits more than fifty specific mental events and at least eight dif-

ferent states of consciousness, yet even these are just the surface level of mind. We can go beyond consciousness to discover the non-conceptual levels of mind; we can examine all the layers, like removing the petals of a rose. We can look at the mind beyond the substance level (even beyond existence or non-existence) as mind is unimaginably vast.

As we investigate the mind more deeply, we discover that mind itself has no substance. It has no color and no shape, no form, no position, no characteristics, no beginning, and no end. It is neither within nor without, and thus it cannot be pinpointed as this or that. It is not mixed together with other things, yet it is not separate from them. The mind cannot be invented, destroyed, rejected, or accepted. It is beyond reasoning and logical processes, beyond ordinary time and all existence.

As we practice meditation we begin to recognize the tremendous activity that goes on in the mind. We can begin to work with particular thoughts and problems, and as we go through the process of confronting, accepting, suppressing, or changing these, we can gain an understanding about the mind and its workings.

One of the major obstacles to discovering and appreciating the depth and quality of the mind is that we take our minds for granted and do not properly respect them. This respect need not be in an egotistical manner, but it is very important to realize how valuable and precious our minds are. Usually, whenever positive experiences occur to us, we praise the ego rather than the mind, for we consider the ego as the agent of the intellect. Yet, when problems or difficulties occur we blame the mind; we give names to our various neuroses, and accept them as real and as part of the mind, although the mind itself is innocent. This rejection of the mind as something foreign and even harmful to us is not a healthy attitude. We often show great concern for our bodies, beautifying ourselves and creating impressive self-images, yet seldom do we equally appreciate the spectrum, realm, and totality of our minds.

The mind is the source of all knowledge and inspiration. When we become enlightened it is the mind that is enlightened; when we

EXERCISE 17
EVALUATING THE MIND

During meditation, and at other times throughout the day, you can observe the workings of the mind. Watching carefully, you can notice when one state of mind ends and another begins.

1 Sense the subtle vibrations of an emotion stirring into being in the wake of a thought, or catch the precise moment when your mind begins interpreting and evaluating inner experiences, assigning them causes and names such as pressure or contentment, anger or love.

2 When you feel confused, note the confusion. As if you were watching a play, you can watch how the stream of thoughts gives way to inner dialogues that conflict with one another. There is no need to manipulate this flow of thoughts or change the drama that is unfolding. Watch with interest, even absorption, but stay detached from the impulse to respond.

3 The mind may begin thinking about meditation itself, wondering if it is being done "right" or straining to remember specific instructions. When this happens, note the tendency of the mind to fixate on specifics that lead to complications and uncertainty. Watch thoughts calmly, without wishing them away or adding to the unfolding mental commentary.

4 Remind yourself that thoughts are insubstantial and changeable, and encourage productive thoughts. Let go of those that cause unnecessary pain. Transform the most negative thoughts and feelings into opportunities for self-understanding and change. Even neurotic thoughts that used to nag you with complaints and self-blame can arise and pass without upsetting your deeper equanimity. Thoughts become allies, bearing accurate information about our perceptions and transmitting warm feelings infused with a gentle awareness.

are sad it is mind that is sad. As we begin to appreciate and respect our minds, we find that mind itself can transform our daily experience. Our problems appear less real—for we discover that all our problems are actually self-created. The more we investigate our minds, the more we go beyond problems, beyond words and concepts, to discover truth. We need not blindly follow anyone else's ideas, but can explore our own minds to greater depth. The career of the meditator moves through three phases. In the first we begin to see how the mind functions, how thoughts, feelings, and sensations rise and fall. The mind becomes calm and disciplined. This harmonious, balanced state is the goal of many meditators. Those who seek appropriate guidance and persevere in their efforts reach the second stage, when the meditator sees that both positive and negative are manifestations of the mind, and that much of his experience is the mind's creation. Finally, in the third stage, the ordinary mind is completely transcended, and Mind emerges, like the sun breaking through clouds, radiant and open.

FINDING SILENCE

To understand who we are and what we are doing, we must understand the meaning of silence. Within silence there is balance—mind and body become transparent, and we can discover who we really are. When everything becomes simplified through silence, all the tangles of our inner knots and problems gradually dissolve. True silence comes from within. It is not merely the absence of speech: it is pure naturalness—absolutely calm, without fixation, without preparation. Nothing is required except, simply, to be.

DISSOLVING THE MIND

Mind itself has no substance. It has no color and no shape. It has no form, no position, no characteristics, no beginning. It is neither within nor without; it cannot be discovered as this or that thing; it is not mixed together with other things, yet is not apart from them. This mind cannot be discovered, invented, destroyed, rejected, or accepted. It is beyond reasoning and so-called logical processes. Discriminating awareness and intuition can lead us to the door of this unoriginated awareness, but through the door is a vastness beyond all that can be expressed—a vastness that can only be entered nakedly, for it is natural, spontaneous openness, without beginning and without end, beyond time and beyond all existence.

This mind, in the absence of conditions, is without memory and association. It is like muddy water, which becomes pure by itself when left undisturbed. When there is no mind, no minding, no intellect, no sensation, no perception, no memory, and no association, what precisely is the mind of a sentient being? "Sentient being" can be spoken of only as long as these function-events are operating.

Normally our ideas depend almost entirely on images shaped by our habitual ways of seeing, hearing, sensing, and responding. Thus we tend to carry on the same patterns of inadequacy or confusion and continue to experience these patterns according to an inner network of interpretations that we always have done. This type of functional knowledge, while helpful when we wish to accumulate information, is useless if it merely reinforces premises that fall apart under investigation. It is like a stream that eventually dries up if it is not supplied by a fresh undercurrent or natural spring. Discriminating, judging, and categorizing our experiences and perceptions into subject and object, seer and seen, solidifies our separateness and results in a lifeless trickle of actions that perpetuate frustration.

Inner clarity develops once we stop trying to cover over, hide from, or escape dealing honestly with daily experiences. We begin to accept things as they are, without trying to reconstruct them to fit some idealized or conceptualized pattern, or force things and people to satisfy our self-image. Suddenly, there is no "one" to defend and no "thing" to hide.

Throughout this inner development, it is important to remember that there is no need to support or maintain a fixed center. As long as there is space, a bird can fly on and on, almost for ever. Similarly, as much as you are able, as long as there is free space, keep yourself open and keep going on. Do not step back or retrace your steps. If you say, "How's my meditation?" the meditation experience disappears.

In Tibet people who mine for gold are constantly looking back at what they have just dug up. They continually evaluate their efforts, wanting to check, "How much did we get? How good is it?" Similarly, the urge to evaluate the quality of our meditation is very strong. Instead of thinking, "Oh, how wonderful my meditation was," or, "Oh, I'm having all sorts of problems," just keep going on. In the space between thoughts are all sorts of openings. Once you enter them, you will not find any center. You will find nothing to hold on to, nothing to point to and say, "That's it!"

Pretend for a moment that all the planets, stars, meteorites, black holes, gaseous nebula—all objects in the heavens—have completely disappeared. What is left is empty space. No inside, no outside: there is nothing that can be stood upon or pointed at.

There is no gravity, no direction, no position, and no judgment. Where in this openness can a center be found?

Dual-mind constantly finds its support in identifying with external objects. But its way of "identifying" is to view some "one" as related to some "thing." The self becomes the subject, and everything else the object. By dividing and categorizing all aspects of experience, by labeling experience as "my" and referring to all perceptions and possessions as "mine," dual-mind establishes its own reality and prevents us from seeing the world as it is. But when the mind loses its hold on any concept or idea—good thought, bad thought, right way, wrong way, true gold, fool's gold—there is no judgment, no loss, and no gain. Personal identity falls away because the concept of identity no longer operates.

Once we completely transcend our subjective viewpoint, our recognizable identity or self-image disappears, as though we were stepping away from a mirror. When self-reflecting identity vanishes, there is no projector and no projection—there is nothing left to project or anyone to project it. Initially we may feel deeply threatened by the notion of losing our sense of identity, but that fear of loss is really a manifestation of the ego's residues: fear is the ego's greatest protector. But at the same time that we lose everything—

completely surrender and give up—we are still totally functional. We are "reborn." We have a new awareness. But the awareness that now sustains us is not samsaric. It operates without predispositions, without taking a position, without identifying anything, without making things solid or fixed. Within this completely open and awakened awareness, everything functions in a new, fresh, open, and positive way.

It is possible that all our perceptions will someday become transmuted into the nature of Buddha-mind. It is also possible for mind itself to disappear. At present it is only our fixations or beliefs, or need for something solid that tricks us into thinking that mind exists. What we believe to be mind is not really mind, for whenever we say "mind is this" or "mind is that," we are immediately lost in some fantasy, conceptualization, or description of mind. But if we experience meditation properly, we will eventually understand that mind itself is totally empty, without content. Therefore, there is nothing we can point to and call "mind." To say that mind is nothing is still an attempt to describe or define mind according to some conception. But as soon as speech begins, meditation is interrupted. This is why silence is so important. Words and concepts can only point to interpreted fragments of our experience, but in silence, awareness comes alive.

Still, there is no way we can directly talk about or illustrate the nature of mind itself. Mind is not an abstraction or the product of some summation. Mind is absolutely structureless. A big rope cannot go through the eye of a needle, but a very fine thread passes through easily. Similarly, when we let go of our concepts of mind, we can go more easily into the gap between thoughts, and enter an infinite and vast space—an openness with no identity.

FINDING THE SPACE
BETWEEN THOUGHTS

When we are able to still our body, breath, and mind, a very comfortable, soothing feeling naturally arises. As we expand this feeling, we find that we feel very much at home there, and we can return to this feeling again and again in daily meditation. We may begin by practicing for  just a few minutes each day. Eventually, however, as we extend these periods, we find that we can meditate effortlessly. And through repeated contact with this feeling, our concentration develops naturally. Our progress can be hindered, however, if we try to interpret these feelings intellectually. For the thought process itself separates us from the experience.

Our thoughts are so much a part of us that even when we are meditating we tend to accept the world of ideas and concepts as our reality. We limit ourselves to this familiar realm, and therefore limit our meditation. We see this effect clearly when we closely examine the nature of thoughts.

When a thought arises in the mind, we "attach" ourselves to it as if it were our child. We feel ourselves as a mother to our thoughts—but this is actually a trick that our minds play on us. In fact, if we watch carefully and try to remain unattached, we can see that each thought arises and passes away without substantial connection to the succeeding one. Thoughts tend to be erratic, to leap from one thing to another, like kangaroos. Each thought has its own character. Some are slow and others fast; one thought may be very positive and the next very negative. Thoughts are just passing through, like cars passing by on the highway. In very rapid succession, one thought comes forth as the last one fades.

As one thought leads to the next, it seems that they have some direction, but despite the sense of motion, there is no genuine progression. Mental events—thoughts—are like a motion picture: although there is a sense of continuity, continuity itself is an illusion created by the projection of a series of similar—but actually individual—images.

As a particular thought or idea arises, it begins to take on form, just like a baby growing in the womb. It develops for a while inside us; then suddenly it is "born" as a fully-shaped idea. As soon as the thought emerges, it cries out; we need to take care of it. Thoughts are difficult and demanding, and we need to learn to handle them properly.

Milarepa's Cave

"When the yogi Milarepa was living in a cave, his single possession was a clay bowl in which he cooked nettles. Two hunters who had seen the smoke from his fire came to the cave at night to steal some food. When they began to search the cave, Milarepa laughed and said, 'I am a yogi, and during the day I can find little to eat. How do you expect to find anything at night? This is a dark, empty place—there is nothing to take away.' "

When the mind is still, thoughts are like drawings on water—before we finish drawing, they flow away. Some people can see a thought when it arises, and then, like snow in California, it is gone before it touches the ground. When we meditate our mind should be like Milarepa's cave—uncluttered. In the same manner, when we do not let our minds fill with thoughts, negative forces will have nothing to grasp, and so they cannot be of harm to us.

By watching our thoughts carefully, we can learn to directly experience each thought or concept as it arises. By gently and skillfully staying with each thought, we can experience the different patterns and tones. This is what is meant by going to the inner experience or by actually becoming the experience. Reaching it is like diving deep into the ocean. On the surface there may be waves, but deep within, there is a profound peace and equilibrium.

This space between thoughts is like the interval between this moment and the future: this thought is gone, but the future one is not yet. In fact this presence of awareness is not involved with past or future; it is not even involved with our usual idea of the present. Contacting this space is like taking a trip to another world, and the quality of the experience is far different from the quality of experience that we ordinarily meet with.

Once we find this space between thoughts, we can expand it into a deep and full experience. As we expand the calm of the space between thoughts, the mind gradually loses its restlessness, and the natural state of mind begins to reveal itself. At first this state is hard to maintain, because our mind still tends to be distracted by thoughts. But as we develop interior balance, our mind gravitates more easily to a deeper level of awareness. When we learn to sustain this awareness for longer and longer periods, it becomes like an internal light, always radiant. We can expand this calm beyond our bodies, beyond even this world, and can feel the vastness, the centerlessness of open space. Our experience becomes alive, fresh, clear, and positive. The more deeply we enter into this space between thoughts, the more powerful our experience.

Within the space between thoughts we see that mind itself is space; transparent and formless. We see that our thoughts, too, are without form. Once we directly experience this sense of openness and space, we are no longer confined in the boxes of concepts, words, and images that have previously restricted our experience.

When images come into your mind, bypass them. Stay with the energy, the seeingness quality, of the thought itself. Again feel out an opening that is part of the thought, an empty place. See this opening, expand it. In this "seeing" time it is important also to listen. In this way we feel as though we were hearing with our eyes; the seeing quality becomes a hearing quality when we keep the eyes loose and relaxed. Now stay in that place. At the instant that thoughts and concepts come, try to see their quality of aliveness.

Every single thought has a nucleus of energy, a center of power and awareness that we can easily find once we put aside the ideas of doing or achieving. The energy in the center just opens. This is being. Being needs no improvements; it needs no doing or moving. Being is not past, not future, not even present. Yet we can expand this state of awareness. First find the small gaps, the little points of entry you will learn to recognize. Then make these gaps bigger, until they fill the whole. At first you will find you are watching, relating to the situation. Later you can engage the total body, and mind; everything becomes a part of the awareness. You can expand it beyond your body, beyond the room. There are no limits. You are one with your experience. That is the meditation practice: expanding, contracting, and expanding again this state of awareness.

This pristine awareness belongs to nothing whatsoever, not to us, not to any place or any time. No one owns it. It is completely open, a new dimension. This universal level of awareness includes everything—individual consciousness embraces all consciousness. Nothing is rejected or excluded; all is clear: we become balanced.

As this intrinsic awareness is expanded, we find that we act harmoniously in each life situation. No longer hampered by conceptions of how things should be, we can be effective in ways that were undreamed of. Being in unity with each situation, we respond in total harmony. Our awareness has a dynamic quality, balancing us in a way that allows our energies to flow freely and smoothly. In this deeply relaxed, meditative state we enter into the full richness and depth of experience. This is the beauty and the potential of being.

EXERCISE 18
CATCHING THOUGHTS

The following, separate techniques can make very good starting points for analytical meditation.

1 Observe how many thoughts pass through your head in one hour. Write each of your thoughts down and categorize them into positive, negative, or neutral. Do this every day for at least one week.

2 Pick out one specific thought—this can be any thought you may have, whether negative or positive. Holding it as long as you can, think about it; do not let it go. There should be no second thought—just concentrate on the one single thought. Do not try to judge it, locate it, or see how it is, but just let it be. When that thought is finished, and another comes, again try to do the same thing—and again try to see how long you can hold one thought. Do this four or five times during the day.

The Spade Sage

 "Once upon a time, near a great city in India, lived a gardener called the Spade Sage. He was called this because everywhere he went he carried his only possession, a garden spade. Using only this spade, he earned a living growing pumpkins, cucumbers, radishes, lettuces, and many other vegetables on a small patch of ground.

One day the Spade Sage thought, 'Though my garden is good and my vegetables are the best, I am not happy. I must give up my spade and go into the forest to become a hermit. I must try to discover the secret of happiness which is locked within my own mind.' So, leaving his spade and his garden behind, he set out for the forest.

Before long, however, the Spade Sage became restless and longed for his old life. He thought about his spade and his little garden so often that he finally admitted to himself, 'This idea of mine was a foolish one. I can only think of my old home and my old habits. I will never find the secret of happiness this way.' So he returned to digging and weeding.

But shortly, be realized that he had been wrong to leave the forest, for he was still not happy. He thought, 'For the sake of one spade and a few vegetables, I have given up my chance to find the secret of happiness locked within my own mind. Tomorrow I will return to the forest and again become a hermit.' But even the Spade Sage himself did not know how great was his desire for the world of men. Even after he had gone to the forest a second time, his spade and his garden called him back to his old life. Indeed, he left his his garden and then returned to it again six more times.

At last he said to himself, 'This is foolishness. I am a poor man. Yet I cannot give up my one and only possession to find the secret of happiness that is within my own mind. Before I leave this time, I will throw my spade into the river where I can never find it.'

At the edge of the water he shut his eyes so he could not see where the spade would fall; then, spinning around three times, he cast his spade into the river. Filled with relief and joy, he began to shout in a loud voice that echoed through the hills like the roar of a lion: 'I have conquered! I have conquered!'

His cries were heard by a king who was returning home victorious after a great battle. Upon meeting him, the king asked, 'Sir, you say that you have conquered. I myself am a conqueror, and I have a great army. But whom have you conquered?'

'Good king,' said the sage, 'a thousand of your victories are nothing compared to mine. You have conquered only other men. I have conquered my own desire.' In that instant the Spade Sage looked within his mind. Freed from attachment to his spade, he found the secret of happiness and became able to teach it to others."

Although the Spade Sage understood that happiness lay within his own mind and not among his possessions or everyday life, it took great courage and faith in himself for him to let go of his attachments and live only within the openness and balance of his mind. Through meditation we too can reflect on the nature of attachments: how they bind us and limit our ability to realize the beauty and joy of inner freedom. While we may not choose to live as hermits, we can develop the strength of mind to free ourselves of bondage to habits and desires. Like the Spade Sage, we can conquer.

USING VISUALIZATION

Visualization is very helpful in the development of awareness, concentration, and clarity. By focusing our consciousness on specific images or symbols, we can loosen the mental constructs that define and limit our perceptions. We thus become open to wider dimensions of experience and also become less vulnerable to our emotions.

In more advanced meditation, when we are no longer so bound by subjects and objects, visualization can take place without form or structure. But as it takes a while before we learn to free our minds from dependence on dualistic thinking, when we are just beginning to develop concentration and visualization, it is useful to focus on specific objects, shapes, or colors.

Traditionally, both concentration and visualization start with focusing on a symbolic letter; they then move on to various symbols, images, mandalas, and deities, each with specific ornaments and qualities. We begin the process by concentrating on whatever we are visualizing for periods of ten or twenty minutes each day, until we have visualized the object of our practice for a total of forty or fifty hours. As we look at the image very loosely, with our eyes completely relaxed and our breath and body very still, very receptive, the image eventually merges with our awareness.

Sometimes when we are just beginning our visualization practice, we may visualize well—but after a while the image may become unsteady or disappear altogether. More often, however, visualization is difficult at first, but as we continue, the image becomes more clearly focused and the visualization improves. Even then we may find that, when we try to visualize a specific image, a different image appears; and this can be disturbing. So we need to practice patiently, for it takes time to perfect these abilities.

A visualization first appears in front of us as though we were looking through a long tunnel or expandable tube. Although this seeing or awareness is very flexible, often we forget the image or become unconscious of it, so we are not able to perform the visualization accurately. Sometimes, however, when we close our eyes, what we are visualizing is just perfectly "there." Such a visualization does not need to be constructed piece by piece in the way that a carpenter builds a house; it arises spontaneously—a perfect image. Once we see it we do not need to change anything. We can just let it be. And this spontaneity is the seed of visualization.

You might ask, "Are visualization and imagination the same?" The answer is that they do have some similarities. But, imagination

EXERCISE 19
SEEING BLUE

Anything can be the subject of a visualization. The important thing is to open your awareness to make your mental image as vivid as possible.

1 Try to inwardly visualize the healing color of turquoise blue—if you cannot see it, feel that you see it. This seeing is beautiful, so just accept it; and this acceptance will help you see it.

2 If you still do not see it, gently convince yourself that you are seeing perfectly, beautifully, and although you still may not see anything, feel the quality and the magnitude of the experience. Stay within the moment and the visualization will eventually come to you.

is like memory or a mental projection, while visualization becomes spontaneous and is like seeing three-dimensionally in all directions. Visualization is a finer, more highly developed, dynamic process. In imagination we can never quite contact the original brilliance of colors, shapes, sounds, and tastes—but visualizations are sometimes so sharp and radiant that they transcend our ordinary perceptions. In the field of visualization no object is mundane.

As we begin our visualization practice, the image is generally just a pale outline; gradually we can learn to focus the color and form more sharply. It is difficult to sharpen the complete visualization all at once, but gradually the colors become very vivid and clear—the light spectrum appears as rich and electrical color—and figures emerge not as lifeless images but as living forms.

As our abilities improve our visualizations can be very complex—with many images becoming one, or one image becoming many. We can develop one single image or mandala to include the entire universe—everything fitting perfectly together. And we can begin to understand the nature of all existence and all

phenomena—time, space, and knowledge. During visualization we may have extraordinary experiences, inexplicable by the rational mind, but we know that what we are seeing is true, because we are experiencing the harmonious working of natural laws.

In visualization we first look at form and color, but later on the image enters our minds naturally, spontaneously. At first we just watch the image as part of our meditation or concentration, but with practice, we can eventually train our minds so that we can see the image within ourselves. Later, we will not even need to look at a picture or close our eyes, and still we will see the image. It comes alive within our awareness.

In practicing visualization we see with awareness, not eyes, and so what we "see" appears differently than in ordinary sight. Although we begin by seeing an image or picture in a certain way, as we develop our visualization the exact form of the image does not matter, because the quality of "seeingness" continues. The image itself is transcended, while awareness nourishes our mind and feelings; this awareness brings more meaning to our daily lives.

The purpose of visualization is to develop our awareness so that wherever we go or whatever we do, we become very mindful, and alert, like a deer's ear. Once we are familiar with the visualization process, we can compare our experience with our ordinary process of perception, and in this way gather information on how better to understand ordinary waking reality. We can arouse our awareness to see how delusion operates within the mind; we can develop this awareness to perceive all knowledge within our consciousness. So visualization adds a new dimension to our perception of the world and gives us a new perspective with which to view our ordinary reality.

USING A MANDALA

The Sanskrit word *mandala* suggests both origin and its infinite continuity. It is linked to the words *mantra* and *manas* (an aspect of mind), and thus to speech and realization. As the perfect field of realization, the mandala arrives at no final point that can be touched; it has no root that can be unearthed; and it displays no edge whose location can be discovered. Like mind, the mandala allows for infinite manifestations, while remaining open and unclaimed. There is nothing in it of substance, nothing that can be traced or designed. As beings bound to particular forms and formulations, we cannot conceive of what is thus unlimited and ultimate, yet still the mandala is available.

Human beings and this planet share five elements: water, earth, air, fire, and space. These five support all life. Sound communicates through space to the ears, and light to the eyes; fragrances are carried on the wind to the nose; food travels through the body via water. Senses and objects interact and merge together, objects presenting themselves to awareness through light. This interaction itself can lead to balance or imbalance, depending on how we respond to the esthetic of nature.

Esthetic balance is the characteristic of the mandala. It symbolizes the structure of reality in distinctive components, which together give the whole its characteristics. Based on ancient knowledge of universal correspondences, the mandala integrates shapes and colors with the elements and the points of the compass in a symmetrical representation of universal harmony. Recognizing the mandala pattern of experience elicits the full potential of being.

The modern world has lost touch with the knowledge of the mandala, which has now become difficult to transmit and explain. But we can glimpse the principle of the mandala in art and nature: the balanced symmetry between center and surrounding field, and the wholeness inherent in beauty. Our consciousness responds to beautiful, balanced forms through communication with the five senses. This response itself exhibits the connectedness between the inner and outer—part of the communication of the mandala.

EXERCISE 20

MEDITATING ON THE MANDALA OF A FLOWER

The flower is similar in form to a mandala, a central point surrounded by petal-like gateways opening out into the four directions, a symbol of consciousness in space and time.

1 Sit comfortably. Breathe slowly and evenly through both your nose and mouth. Place a flower in front of you, and relax your eyes. Try not to stare at the flower, gently rest your gaze upon it; almost look "through" it— even imagine that the flower looks back at you.

2 Consider how the outermost petals of the flower are like past memories; the inner, future concerns. The center is like the present, where subject and object interact. If we take care in the present, the past and future will be accommodated. Growth naturally arises out of this caring presence.

CHAPTER 4

TEACHING AND ENLIGHTENMENT

finding help with your practice

The spiritual path has many obstacles, such as our inner dialogues, our feelings, our worries, or even our friends or families. So, good influences are crucial. Once we are interested in the spiritual path, associating with those of a similar nature can help support and protect us, and can create less confusion for us. It is difficult to find a qualified teacher, and equally difficult to accept the responsibilities of being a good student. These do not mean simply to work hard, but also to be receptive, open, and devoted to the teacher.

In this chapter we explore the importance of sustaining practice through difficult times, as well as looking at how to find the right teacher to guide us on the path toward deeper awareness. We also look at how we can open our hearts and minds to our teacher, and receive their wisdom willingly and non-judgmentally in a spirit of honesty and devotion.

SUSTAINING YOUR PRACTICE

When beginning this quest we may simply ask questions and look closely at others to see what they know, to see if they have anything to offer that can help us make sense of things. Soon, however, we discover that this method of looking is limited. Others may give us helpful advice, but we can gain certainty only through our own experience, by a process of self-discovery.

Meditation provides the key for unlocking the secrets of our mind, as well as the means to relieve human suffering. This sounds wonderfully promising; the thought that our practice can bring understanding and happiness seems to provide all the inspiration we will ever need. But when we have just begun to meditate, this kind of motivation has not been tested by any challenges. It is mostly an idea, and thus rather easy to maintain. After we meditate for a while, conflicts, doubts, and frustrations may arise; then our motivation must move to a deeper level, a level of action rather than mere intention.

Many people find that the initial stage of meditative practice intensifies previously concealed mental attitudes and traits. Resistance, anger, boredom, and other negative habit patterns come into awareness. When these feelings surface in meditation, we can be overwhelmed by anxiety and doubt about the actual benefits of practice. We may be bored, have trouble staying awake during meditation, or suddenly remember something else we have to do. We may not practice for weeks or even months. Though we recognize the value of meditation, we may come to feel that it is in conflict with other aspects of our life: for example, we might often have to choose between practice and entertainment or social contact. Perhaps the biggest obstacle to our progress is a sense that these conflicts make us ill-suited for meditation. If we take this

feeling seriously, it can lead us to stop meditating altogether.

It is a rare individual who does not encounter these and many other difficulties when beginning to practice—and it is especially important during these times to persevere. Read good books that can help you to understand your practice more deeply; encourage yourself to look at your life and meditation in fresh ways. Keep alive your purpose in practicing; know that however unpleasant or difficult these experiences may be, they are part of the truth you seek. Rather than closing your eyes and turning away from them, look more deeply and try to understand the truth unfolding in your life. Give yourself time and space to fully appreciate what is happening. Great calm and clarity may not appear instantaneously, or may last only a short time, but as long as you are patient and motivated to practice, these qualities will surely be realized.

Even after you have practiced for some time, and meditation comes more easily, you may find yourself feeling numb and dull, or bored with your practice. To transform this mood meditate loosely, yet energetically. Allow your intelligence to guide you, and relax as much as possible, not getting too involved in evaluating your meditation or judging your experience.

When you are faced with conflicts, it may be helpful to talk to a teacher or an experienced friend. A good teacher knows you well and is able to make suggestions that are appropriate to you. Because he has confronted similar experiences on his own path, he can point the way. His understanding is sure and objective, and he can provide momentum when your motivation begins to falter.

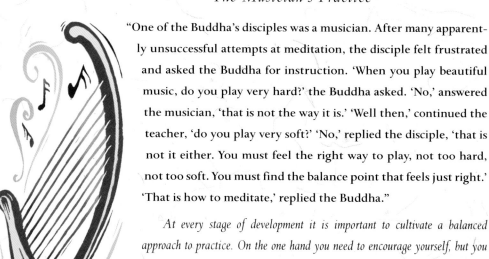

The Musician's Practice

"One of the Buddha's disciples was a musician. After many apparently unsuccessful attempts at meditation, the disciple felt frustrated and asked the Buddha for instruction. 'When you play beautiful music, do you play very hard?' the Buddha asked. 'No,' answered the musician, 'that is not the way it is.' 'Well then,' continued the teacher, 'do you play very soft?' 'No,' replied the disciple, 'that is not it either. You must feel the right way to play, not too hard, not too soft. You must find the balance point that feels just right.' 'That is how to meditate,' replied the Buddha."

At every stage of development it is important to cultivate a balanced approach to practice. On the one hand you need to encourage yourself, but you should also be alert to the possibility that the quality of your motivation will change. If you practice with dedication and patience, meditation will become an integral part of your life. Then you will no longer need to make an effort: meditation will arise naturally, like the morning sun.

FINDING A TEACHER,
BEING A STUDENT

The biographies of the greatest Buddhist masters are filled with stories describing the crucial roles of teachers in their training. Deep appreciation shines forth in the descriptions of how they met their teachers, the trials they faced, the teachings they received, and the realization they gained. The teacher–student relationship is revealed to be as close as that between parent and child.

A relationship this close, and with such far-reaching consequences, is not undertaken lightly. Ashvaghosha, an important early Buddhist poet, wrote: "So that the commitment between the teacher and student will not be broken, there must be mutual examination beforehand to determine whether each can brave a guru–disciple relationship." Before a student chooses a teacher, he must be sure that the teacher is qualified, capable, and compassionate. It is also important that the student feels respect and a sense of empathy toward the teacher. Once the student has made his choice, the teacher will test the student's determination and ability to pursue the spiritual path. Only when mutual trust is established does the teacher formally accept the student. When teacher and student have made their commitments to one another in this way, a bond is formed that can never be broken—only transformed by the realization of enlightenment.

By accepting a student the teacher promises to work wholeheartedly for the well-being of the student, doing everything in his power to ensure the student's physical, mental, and spiritual health. Because of the teacher's wider experience and learning, he has greater responsibility to the student than the student has toward him. Recognizing the depth of the teacher's intentions can help the student develop confidence in the teacher and in the path: then the student can accept the teachings more easily.

Once students begin to follow the teachings, they usually think they will get something in return: a happier life, more friends, greater power. Although it is true that Dharma practice produces many benefits, a student's particular desires may not be fulfilled. These expectations seem reasonable and positive, but they make it difficult to accept the teachings because they color understanding. A student who holds fixed ideas about the teacher or the teachings is like an unclean jar that muddies whatever is poured into it. No matter how pure the teachings the student receives, they are clouded by prejudgment, and cannot be understood clearly.

To help the student let go of his expectations, the teacher will encourage him to look at himself with complete honesty. This may not be easy, as a clear view requires cutting through layers of pride and self-doubt, but the teacher can see through these obscurations.

The teacher offers instructions that can lead to the experiences and understanding he himself has gained. For the student these teachings are a map, and the teacher is a guide. It is the student's role to listen to the guide and to try to follow the map. Although the teacher's oral and written instructions are just ideas and con-cepts, like symbols on a map, they are a means for reaching the destination. If we do not try to follow the directions, realization may not come; we may wander off the path and lose our way.

This kind of commitment, requiring one to persevere for years, even in the absence of visible results, may be difficult to implement in today's world. Particularly in the West, where personal freedom is so highly valued, we may feel threatened by devotion: trusting someone so completely seems to jeopardize our independence. For this reason, it can be helpful to look at the teacher from another perspective, as a symbol for the clarity and serenity that arise whenever we open our minds. Thus the term guru can refer to our internal awareness, our Buddha nature, and "surrendering to the guru" can mean opening to the enlightened quality of mind.

Milarepa's Learning

"When the great Tibetan yogi Milarepa began to study with his teacher, Marpa, he was given very difficult tasks to accomplish, but the formal spiritual teachings that Milarepa sought were withheld. As Milarepa completed each task, he hoped that at last he would receive the teachings, but not only did Marpa refuse to give the teachings, he had Milarepa destroy his

work and do it over again. After many years had passed in this way, Milarepa began to think he could get the teachings he desired elsewhere. Knowing that the irascible Marpa would not willingly permit him to go, Milarepa left without Marpa's knowledge, and connived his way into being accepted by another teacher who gave Milarepa instructions that guaranteed enlightenment. Still, although Milarepa followed these instructions to the letter, he attained absolutely no result. The new teacher could not understand this—until he discovered that Milarepa had not finished his training with Marpa, and had in fact left without permission. Milarepa was promptly returned to Marpa. Eventually, when Marpa felt that his student was ready, Milarepa did receive the highest teachings, and in time became a supremely realized yogi."

This story illustrates how important it is to trust in your teacher and to maintain a strong commitment to him, even when you do not necessarily understand his methods.

Still we may ask, "Is a personal teacher necessary to attain enlightenment?" The answer depends upon the individual. Most people can benefit from a relationship with an experienced teacher. There are those, however, who find such a relationship a hindrance: their fear of being manipulated blocks the instructions of a teacher. Such people find it easier to digest painful information about themselves at their own pace, on their own initiative. There are also rare individuals who can effectively direct their own development, and do not need a teacher at all.

While a teacher–student relationship may be advisable for most of us, a qualified teacher may not be easy to find. Therefore, it is essential to evaluate any prospective teacher carefully: Does he have a fully enlightened lineage? Is he willing to take responsibility for his students? An authentic teacher–student relationship is different from relationships in which there is dependence or manipulation. A genuine teacher is our true friend, willing to help us to become absolutely free.

TRUST, DEVOTION, AND COMPASSION

The eighteenth-century Tibetan lama Jigmay Lingpa once said, "Although you may have acquired great knowledge and wisdom through years of study and practice, and although you may have learned to be patient and to vigorously practice meditation, still you may be far from attaining enlightenment. One can attain the ultimate realization only through sincere devotion and total trust in the teachings and the teacher." It is very simple. Devotion and compassion can take us very close to absolute reality.

THE ENLIGHTENED TEACHER

The teachings of the path to enlightenment have been passed on from teacher to student in an unbroken lineage reaching back to the Buddha himself. The Buddha taught, and those he taught in turn taught others.

This is the living tradition that maintains the path to enlightenment. Those who pass on the teachings do so by realizing the Buddha's teachings in themselves, and they therefore transmit not only the texts and their true meanings, but also the actual experience of enlightenment.

The masters of the lineage, working on inner levels, can transmit the enlightenment lineage directly—without words or concepts, without even the use of symbolic gestures or expressions. However, it is not easy to receive this transmission; our conceptual minds, our egos which judge and interpret all our experience, get in the way.

In what we usually call teaching, learning is a matter of filtering words and meanings through our conceptual understanding. But in the teachings of the path, because each word is a direct doorway to enlightenment, we need to understand the inner meanings by our direct experience. When our hearts and minds open to these deeper meanings, a teacher can then help us to transcend the limitations that our conceptual minds place on our understanding.

Both intellectual and experiential understanding grow and deepen together. Thus every step in the transmission—the teachings, the texts, and the learning process—must be carried out with utmost care, or the direct path to enlightenment will be obscured. Impatient with our progress, we may feel that the "more" we learn the better off we are. But going from teacher to teacher diffuses our understanding instead of deepening it. We therefore need to carefully select an enlightened guide and then follow him until our understanding becomes deep and clear.

How can we be sure that our teacher will be able to guide us to this realization? With both our intelligence and our intuition as guides, we naturally are attracted to a teacher who has brought to completion those qualities we wish to develop in ourselves. A teacher lives the inner meaning of the teachings, and so we see in him our inner nature. Then, through his enlightened compassion, he helps us to develop our own qualities of compassion, integrity, and inner confidence.

When the teacher is compassionate and open, the path naturally unfolds, and our lives take on an even and flowing quality. Gradually we become more aware of our inner nature, and build up a depth of self-understanding and inner strength.

Yet the teachings do not always come in forms that are pleasing to us or to our egos. A compassionate teacher, in revealing our inner nature to our conscious awareness, also brings out those qualities that we do not like to admit in ourselves. We can get rid of these things once we see them, but these qualities may be such that our egos do not wish to give them up. And our egos, when they feel threatened with loss, may cause us to doubt the teachings and the teacher; they may even lead us to believe that if we do not like a certain teaching, it must certainly be wrong. At this point we may feel impelled to break with the teacher instead of our ego.

But to break with the teacher is to break with our trust in ourselves. By this picking and choosing, accepting and rejecting, we undercut our own development and strengthen only our limitations. In this way we not only invite confusion, but also a profound feeling of guilt and failure, which makes further progress on the path extremely difficult.

Therefore, confidence in the teacher and in what he represents is needed from the start. For the lineage to continue unbroken, there must be mutual trust, openness, honesty, and integrity as the basis of the path. Communities built upon this foundation will continue to prosper, and the future of the lineage will be secure.

The teachings leading to direct experience are the touchstones for the stages of our growth. Finally, we discover that the teachings and our own experience of enlightenment have merged. We have transcended our samsaric nature. Now we see that all nature and all existence are already illuminated.

Once we become enlightened, we become part of the lineage, and share the same living knowledge and understanding of the Buddha. This is the thread of enlightenment. We then carry this on in our own understanding, in our work in the world.

After this experience, no questions or doubts remain: we have understanding of the unbroken lineage. The inspiration of this ancient lineage of enlightenment lives within us, and we are open to the enlightenment nature that is inherent in all existence.

The Goatherd and the Naga

"Once there was a man who herded goats for a living. His work was strenuous, and it always seemed to him that he never had enough to eat, so he got into the habit of stealing the goats' milk before he took the animals home to be milked by their owner. He always made sure to take more than enough, so that he would not be hungry later. Every day he milked the goats, drank what he could, and threw the remainder into the river that flowed by the cave where he took shelter.

Now there was a family of Nagas [powerful beings often represented as half-snake, half-human] who lived in the river, and Nagas love goat's milk. The king of the Nagas thought that whoever would offer so much precious milk must be doing so for a reason, so he appeared one evening to the goatherd and asked, 'For what reason do you offer us this wonderful food?' Said the goatherd, 'I am a very great man; therefore, I feed you.' The Naga replied, 'Dear master, what then can I offer you? I can give you whatever powers you would like.' The goatherd, elated, said, 'I would like to be able to sit in midair; I will then attract many disciples due to my ability.' The Naga replied, 'Fine. I will arrange this for you if you will continue to supply me with goat's milk. Whenever you give teachings you may sit on my back, but I shall remain invisible to everyone else.'

Word spread of the goatherd's ability to sit in midair, and many villagers came to receive teachings from him. Although his teachings made little sense, many people worshiped him because of his 'power.'

When the great Pandit Nagarjuna heard about this goatherd, he came to see him. The Naga, realizing that such an accomplished master as Nagarjuna would be able to see him, quickly ran away, leaving the goatherd to tumble to the ground. Disillusioned and disgusted, all the disciples went away."

Like the goatherd we may seem for a time to gain certain powers or abilities, but power that comes from someone else cannot be relied upon. The real power is the ability to control our minds and emotions, and this can be achieved only by means of our own efforts.

Because the real experience of enlightenment can come only through our own actions, we must make whatever we do contribute to our growth. Even ordinary activities, such as working in the kitchen, offer an opportunity to develop our awareness and our willingness to serve others. There is never a lack of opportunity to test ourselves, to face ourselves, to be honest and sincere. True devotion, trust, and acceptance begin in our own hearts. Later, when we must face difficult situations, we will not forget the teachings of our inner understanding; these difficulties will turn into new opportunities to grow and to awaken inwardly.

NATURAL BEING——
A FINAL WORD

Natural being is our enlightened nature. This being is not something apart from us that we must recapture; we are this being. When we make natural being our spiritual home, truth and beauty arise as spontaneous gifts. Perfect knowledge shines into our lives, and our body, mind, and senses lead us effortlessly toward enlightenment. The spiritual path is as close as our heartbeat.

Although the perfect harmony and ease of natural being are so near, they are often somehow elusive. We frequently have the anxious feeling that we lack something essential to our well-being. We may imagine fulfillment to lie in an ideal existence far away from our normal one, and tire ourselves out searching for it.

Even by attempting to mold our meditation practice into a perfect pattern we can develop habits that keep us from accomplishing our aims. "Oh, this is not the right way to meditate," we say to ourselves. We think we are not getting anywhere and criticize ourselves for lack of progress. But these judgments set up a boundary between us and meditation, and we lose touch with the flowing harmony of our nature. This situation is like being hungry and having nourishing food in the cupboard but not eating it.

So, rather than trying to identify wisdom, awareness, or meditation, rather than worrying about whether your meditation is good or bad, simply acknowledge these thoughts without getting caught in their meaning. You do not need to do anything.

With no subject reaching out and no object to possess, being opens from within. Then you may say, "I can see a subtle difference from my usual experience. I'm excited at this discovery. I want to report it to myself." But the moment you try to express this experience, it is gone. Although you may be trying to preserve the experience, you are only separated once again from natural being.

When such thoughts arise, or when we experience a strong feeling or emotion, we can relax the interpretive side of ourselves. Rather than becoming involved with interpretations, images, or sensations, we can remain with the energy in its pure form. Contacting the energy in this way, we may see that it touches the wholeness of being, like a raindrop falling into the ocean. Then we have found the way to convert our thoughts and emotions into meditative experience, opening the mind to the play of being.

The more we participate in natural being, the less we need special techniques and the less we worry about finding answers to our questions. The wider our concept of the mind becomes, the more experience we accept without judgment. This acceptance itself becomes meditation, and we realize that meditation is an integral part of our experience. Everything that is precious, true, and beautiful is within natural being, so there is no need to look for special experiences or insights, or to report to the mind on what has happened. When we are in touch with our inner nature, the distinction between meditative and non-meditative states dissolves.

Becoming attuned to natural being makes life truly interesting. Dullness and boredom no longer arise. Whatever we see, hear, taste, or feel—whatever comes to us in life—becomes rich and alive. Life is interesting because, whether or not we succeed fully in what we intend, we always enjoy and appreciate our efforts.

A joyful, balanced way of living is our natural response to being. Our hearts open to others. Honesty and appreciativeness become our essential morality, and we do not complicate our life situations by insincerity or manipulation. We no longer create negative patterns, so further problems will not arise in the future. In this way, we move gradually toward enlightenment.

ABOUT THE NYINGMA INSTITUTE

Based in Berkeley, California, the Nyingma Institute is a secular education center, where members of the public can investigate the teachings of Tibetan Buddhism and explore the applications of those teachings to Western lifestyles. Founded in 1972 by Tarthang Tulku, the Institute offers a full range of classes, workshops, and retreats in Meditation, Nyingma Psychology, Kum Nye (Tibetan yoga), Tibetan Language, and the principles of Buddhist teachings.

A recognized leader in teaching meditation to the West, the Nyingma Institute offers an extensive range of meditation classes, workshops, and retreats. Silent sitting, walking meditation, and mantra practice are some of the rich meditative practices offered. Every course, regardless of subject, includes study of meditation.

The qualities of mind developed through meditation are a necessary basis for progress in all areas of Buddhist study. The Institute emphasizes Analytical Meditation in Nyingma Psychology courses, where students study the nature of consciousness, identify patterns of thought, feeling, and emotion, and examine the connection between "inner" and "outer" experience. The Institute presents methods to promote incisive awareness of mental events, together with techniques to transform negative mental patterns, sustain the dynamic of meditation, and bring the benefits of meditation into daily life. An extensive program of Buddhist Studies covers the therapeutic applications of Buddhist teachings, and progresses to an in-depth study of the *Sutras* (the Buddha's teachings), the *Abhidharma* (the study of mind), and the works of some of the great Buddhist philosophers. Residential programs include a four-month Human Development Training Retreat and a two-month Integration Retreat. These are designed to activate inner resources, revitalize the psyche, and bring balance to all aspects of life.

CONTACTING THE INSTITUTE

Nyingma Institute
1815 Highland Place, Berkeley,
CA 94707, US
Tel: 001 510 843 6812
Fax: 001 510 486 1679

Nyingma Centrum Nederland
(founded 1989)
Reguliersgracht 25, 1017 LJ,
Amsterdam, Netherlands
Tel: 00 31 20 620 5207
Fax: 00 31 20 622 7143

Instituto Nyingma do Brasil
(founded 1989)
Rua Cayowaa 2085 – Sumaré,
01285-011 São Paolo, Brazil
Tel: 00 55 11 3864 4785
Fax: 00 55 11 3673 0292

Nyingma Zentrum Deutschland
(founded 1989)
Siebachstrasse 66, Köln, Germany
Tel: 00 49 221 589 0474

Centro Nyingma do Rio de Janeiro (founded 1996)
Rua Casuarina 297, Casa 2, Rio de
Janeiro RJ, CEP 22260-160, Brazil
Tel: 00 55 21 2527 9388
Fax: 00 55 21 2579 1066

FURTHER READING

Nyingma Psychology Series
The following books are authored by Tarthang Tulku and published by Dharma Publishing (Berkeley, California). They present the core teachings of the Nyingma Institute: *Reflections on Mind*; *Gesture of Balance*; *Openness Mind*; *Kum Nye Relaxation Parts 1 & 2*; *Skillful Means*; *Hidden Mind of Freedom*; *Knowledge of Freedom*

Translations of Buddhist Works on Meditation (Dharma Publishing)
Longchenpa *Kindly Bent to Ease Us, Parts I–III* (transl. Herbert V. Guenther), 1976. A guide to the Dzogchen path to enlightenment
Mipham, Lama *Calm and Clear* (transl. with a commentary by Tarthang Tulku), 1973. Two practical guides to meditation by a leading 19th-century master and scholar.

INDEX

A

acceptance 67
advice 142, 144
    see also teachers
Amitabha 99
anxiety 34, 42, 54–5, 70
Ashvaghosha 145
attachment(s) 74
    letting go of 72, 74, 132–3
attitudes 45
Avalokiteshvara,
    Bhodhisattva 99
avoidance 34–9, 44
awareness 12, 55, 60, 74–9,
    100
    accessibility 54
    checking 28
    developing 29, 30
    in everyday life 33, 42, 82,
        98
    expanding 106–8, 110–11,
        129–31
    mantras and 98
    mind and 119
    mirror exercise 37
    as natural state 65
    pressure and 72, 106
    relaxation and 106, 109

B

balance 39, 55, 61–8, 89,
    90–91, 112, 115, 130
    mandalas and 138–9
    silence and 122
being 130
beliefs 26, 59
body 86–9, 92–3
    balancing 90–91
    music of 47
    see also exercises
body centers 87, 88–9
body of energy 56–7
body pattern 87–9
boredom 21, 143
breathing 87–9, 94–5

expanding awareness
    through 106, 109
Buddha, the 8, 18–19, 144,
    149
    teachings of 20, 22
Buddha-mind 126
Buddhism 17
    tradition of 149, 151
    see also Dharma

C

change 58–60
    attitudes to 35–8
    positive 67
    see also impermanence
chanting 96
    see also mantras
choice 66–8
clouds 82
color 135, 136
commitment 29, 39, 104
communication 37
compassion 50–53
concentration 115, 134
    on body centers 89
    expanding 110
confidence 26, 29, 30–31
consciousness 119
    see also mind
contradictions 67

D

death 16, 32, 41
Dharma 17, 20, 98
difficulties *see* problems
disappointment 16, 17
dreams 58, 116–17
dualism 26–7, 78, 81–2, 125

E

ego 39, 51, 78, 120, 125,
    150–51
elements 138
emotions *see* feelings
emptiness 18

see also shunyata
energy 28, 64, 65–6, 86–9
    developing 109
    pure 108, 155
    relaxation and 106
    of thoughts 130
    three elements of 87–9
energy centers 87, 88–9
    breath and 94
enjoyment 32–3
enlightenment 9, 151
    teaching and 149–51
    see also natural being
etheric body 88
exercises, physical 56–7,
    90–91, 106, 110–11
experience(s) 80–83, 102–3
    appreciating 70
    learning from 8–9
    meditation and 13, 14, 26
    mind and 118, 122
    mindfulness and 105
    "peak" 28
    "psychic" or "mystic" 76–7,
        108
    reliving 102
    shifting perception of 67,
        103
    see also senses

F

fear 35, 40–41
feelings 28–9, 61–4
    changing 67
    expanding 106–8
    responsibility for 45
    self-healing for 63
fighters 30
flexibility 67
flowers 117, 139
flying 76, 113
focusing 134
    see also concentration *and*
    visualization
future 33, 139

ACKNOWLEDGMENTS

With sincere appreciation for the work of everyone at Duncan Baird Publishers, **Dharma Publishing** would like to acknowledge the vision of Duncan Baird, without whose patience and perseverance this book would not have come into being. We thank Judy Barratt, whose excellent editing and organizing skills gave this book shape and form; Rachel Cross, for her coordination skills, patience, and willingness to accommodate our needs; Matthew Ward, for his skilled figure photography; and Cathie Bleck, for her fine artwork and flexibility.

Duncan Baird Publishers would like to thank everyone at Dharma Publishing and the Nyingma Institute, and especially Elizabeth Cook for her expertise and guidance, and Charaka Jungens for attending the photoshoots. Our thanks also to Matthew Ward (photographer), Jasmine Hemsley (model), and Tinks Reading (make-up artist).